The Practical Peirce

The Practical Peirce

◆

An Introduction to the Triadic Continuum Implemented as a Computer Data Structure

John Zuchero

iUniverse, Inc.
New York Lincoln Shanghai

The Practical Peirce
An Introduction to the Triadic Continuum Implemented as a Computer Data Structure

iUniverse books may be ordered through booksellers or by contacting:

iUniverse
2021 Pine Lake Road, Suite 100
Lincoln, NE 68512
www.iuniverse.com
1-800-Authors (1-800-288-4677)

ISBN: 978-0-595-44112-9 (pbk)
ISBN: 978-0-595-88435-3 (ebk)

Printed in the United States of America

This book is dedicated to my consistently supportive wife Sandy, the educator; my decidedly imaginative son Brad, the scientist; my fictively creative son, Andrew, the storyteller, and to the memory of my mother who was always ready to listen to my stories.

I'd also like to thank Jane Mazzagatti for her eloquence in explaining her theories to me, and for her time, help, and patience in "hammering out the hammer marks" of this shared endeavor.

Contents

Acknowledgements

As solitary as the writing of a book is, it's often the interaction with others that make the information more clear and relevant. I was lucky to have people with whom I was able to ask for help. Hopefully the following is comprehensive, but please accept my apologies if I missed anyone—the memory isn't what it was.

I'd like to thank Barbara Geraghty, Carol Giblin, Shelby Moore, Pete Mazzagatti, and David Zuchero for reading early drafts of the chapters. Also thanks to Jane Claar for her critical reading of many of the more complex topics.

I'd also like to thank Marc Rosenberg for creating the market basket example that I used to explain associations and to David Zuchero for providing the clinical trial example. Jane Claar and Steve Rajcan provided me with assistance in understanding the probability of Texas Hold'em—I hope they do well the next time they're in Vegas.

The advent of the Internet and the Web is truly a benefit for someone researching information on Charles Peirce. While writing this book I came across a number of nice people who were willing to share their expertise and time with me. Professor Sara Barrena of the University of Navarra provided me with help regarding the Calderoni transcript, as well as reading the final draft from a Peircian philosophical perspective. Thanks also to Rob Cross, a professor of management at the University of Virginia and Research Director of The Network Roundtable, who gave me permission to use the fictitious organization chart that I used to explain K clusters. And thanks to Judith Rosen, the daughter of the late theoretical biologist Robert Rosen, for clarifying my long outdated knowledge of biological classification.

And finally, there are two people whom I'd like to thank. The first is my editor Delores Peterson, who actually volunteered to edit my final draft. Please note that any remaining grammatical errors are purely my fault—I'm sure she caught them, I just missed them. The second person is Jane Mazzagatti who gave me the opportunity to become the external voice of her amazing rediscovery and invention—thanks again Jane.

Preface

The writer of a book can do nothing but set down the items of his thought. For the living thought, itself, in its entirety, the reader has to dig into his own soul. I think I have done my part, as well as I can. I am sorry to have left the reader an irksome chore before him. But he will find it worth the doing. Charles Peirce[1]

The effect of pragmatism here is simply to open our minds to receiving any evidence, not to furnish evidence. Charles Peirce[2]

This book is a collaboration between Jane Campbell Mazzagatti and myself. Mazzagatti is a senior software engineer at Unisys Corporation. Jane and I met in 1997 when we worked on the same research and development project, she as a principal software engineer and I as an instructional designer and technical communicator. In early 2000 our paths diverged, but we reconnected in 2005 when she recruited me to join her on a new project that had sprung out of research she had conducted during the previous years. This book is based on my interviews with Mazzagatti over the course of a two-year period from February 2005 through February 2007. In this book, whenever I use the word "we," I am referring to Mazzagatti and myself.

You'll learn more about Mazzagatti in later chapters; however it is important to understand from the beginning that this book is about two different, yet related ideas. First, it is about a practical invention, an invention that Mazzagatti conceived of, implemented, and patented as a new and unique computer data structure. This unique structure, which she called the "Triadic Continuum," is based on her interpretation of the writings of Charles Sanders Peirce. It's important to note that this invention is not simply a theoretical construct, but a breakthrough in data modeling and an actual working computer application, which is currently being used to more efficiently analyze large streaming datasets.

Also note that in this book I have strived to explain the concepts in a straightforward non-technical way, but that the structure of the Triadic Continuum is new, evolutionary, and while elegant in its simplicity, somewhat complex. I hope that understanding the concepts does not become, as in Peirce's words in the above quote, "an irksome chore," but I need to stress that you may have to spend some time thinking about what is written without letting any preexisting perceptions influence or cloud your understanding of these new ideas. As Mazzagatti says to you the reader, "you may have to rearrange your neurons, especially if you have preconceived ideas that you have formed through your education, experience, and knowledge." When she says, "Preconceived ideas" she means that some computer scientists may have to suspend preconceived notions of how relational databases are constructed and function. She also means that some Peirce scholars may have to suspend the notion that Peirce was primarily a philosopher and secondarily a scientist. In other words, Mazzagatti and I ask you to read this book with a reflective, flexible, and open mind.

As Mazzagatti and her colleagues learn more about the inherent nature of the structure of the Triadic Continuum, they discover more and more far-reaching implications to fields other than computer science. Therefore, the second fundamental idea of this book deals with a larger implication than that associated with a new computer data structure. This larger implication can be summed up as Mazzagatti's premise that during Charles Peirce's life, he was fascinated with how the human mind reasons and with all of the scientific and philosophical implications of an understanding of the mechanisms of how the structure of the brain records experience, constructs memories, and accesses previously stored experience and knowledge. She believes that the Triadic Continuum explains and illustrates many of Peirce's key theories that deal with human reasoning and the logic of thought. We readily admit that this is a controversial theory. This book was written to explain her theory and to point to some of the correlations between her theory and the theories and intellectual speculations of Charles Peirce.

It is also important to mention that, unlike others, neither Mazzagatti nor I have spent our careers in the study of Peirce. While Mazzagatti conducted doctoral level research on Peirce and has spent much of the last ten years deeply involved in reading and reinterpreting his work, I was introduced to Peirce during a presentation in 1997. I had been asked to write an article on a new computer technology that was based on the work of someone named Charles Peirce. After listening to the presentation I was immediately hooked on the potential of the technology and on this interesting character named Peirce. I eventually joined the project alongside the computer engineers, one of whom was Mazzagatti. During this project, Mazzagatti realized that the design of the proposed technology was flawed. This led her to question the lead scientist's knowledge of Peirce. Without receiving convincing answers, she began her own investigation into Peirce. When the project lost its funding in 1999, Mazzagatti continued her own research, which eventually led to her discovery and invention, both of which led to the establishment of a new project.

We hope that because we are not classically trained Peirce scholars and because the ideas in this book may be controversial, you are not deterred from keeping an open and inquiring mind as you read this book—for as Peirce suggested, "The object of reasoning is to find out, from the consideration of what we already know, something else which we do not know."[3]

How This Book Is Organized

The first chapter of this book explains why we believe that Peirce used all of the tools at his disposal to communicate his theories on human reasoning to the world—as a scientist would—through the use of observation, theory, and experimentation. Following Chapter 1, the next two chapters present background information that we feel some readers may need to understand the Triadic Continuum and how it was used to construct a practical, functioning computer data structure. Chapter 2 is the abbreviated story about how Mazzagatti was introduced to Peirce. Chapter 3 is based on a presentation Mazzagatti gave to non-technical managers whom she was trying to educate on where her invention fit into the world of computing. And so, this chapter provides a brief overview of traditional databases and why knowledge of how they work will help the reader understand the power of the Triadic Continuum.

The middle chapters are a straightforward but technical explanation of the Triadic Continuum and how it can be used as a practical computer application. Chapter 4 explains the Triadic Continuum—the basic triad, sensors, and how the unique interlocking data structure is constructed. It is in Chapter 5 that we explain how this structure was first implemented and patented. Chapter 6 explains a fundamental point in understanding the Triadic Continuum—that one doesn't "find" or "locate" information within the structure, one "realizes" what is already there. Here you'll learn that it is simply a matter of asking the right question to realize the relationships that are inherently associated with the data within the structure. In Chapter 7 we explain the different types of simple relationships that can be realized within the structure. More complex relationships are covered in Chapters 8 through 11. Chapter 8 discusses how classification is easily determined within the Triadic Continuum and how this harks back to Peirce's concept of natural classes. Chapter 9 covers another complex relationship, that of associations. Chapter 10 discusses relationships that show up as patterns over time, which can be used to realize trends in data. And finally, Chapter 11 covers how relationships are realized through the clustering of knowledge within the Triadic Continuum.

The subject of Chapter 12 is probability. Here we show some of the unique features of the commonly misunderstood science of probability as interpreted through the lens of Peirce and an understanding of the Triadic Continuum.

In the final chapter, Chapter 13, we speculate on some of the possible implications of the combination of Peirce's theories, Mazzagatti's reinterpretation of his underlying theories, and her invention of the data structure and its associated software. We also try to illustrate how an understanding of the Triadic Continuum can benefit those in other fields who are also trying to interpret Peirce's work and find the key to unlocking the practical nature of the thought and wisdom of the great American scientist, and philosopher, Charles Sanders Peirce.

1

The Scientist, Charles Sanders Peirce

Thus, in brief, my philosophy may be described as the attempt of a physicist to make such conjecture as to the constitution of the universe as the methods of science may permit, with the aid of all that has been done by previous philosophers. Charles Peirce[1]

I recognize two branches of science: Theoretical, whose purpose is simply and solely knowledge of God's truth; and Practical, for the uses of life. Charles Peirce[2]

It may not be the best idea to begin a book with a lengthy quote; but my intent is to introduce some readers to Charles Sanders Peirce without writing a mini biography. It's also my intent to set the stage for how Peirce is perceived in this book versus how he is perceived by others. So, I've purposely selected the following quote, which I feel gives the necessary background of the man and his work, and highlights the fact that he is perceived primarily as a philosopher and not a practical man of science.

> Charles Sanders Peirce (1839–1914) was the founder of American pragmatism (later called by Peirce "pragmaticism" in order to differentiate his views from others being labeled "pragmatism), a theorist of logic, language, communication, and the general theory of signs (which was often called by Peirce "semeiotic"), an extraordinarily prolific mathematical logician and general mathematician, and a developer of an evolutionary, psycho-physically monistic metaphysical system. A practicing chemist and geodesist by profession, he nevertheless considered scientific philosophy, and especially logic, to be his vocation. In the course of his polymathic researches, he wrote voluminously on an exceedingly wide range of topics, ranging from mathematics, mathematical logic, physics, geodesy, spectroscopy, and astronomy, on the one hand, to psychology, history, and economics, on the other.[3]

The name Charles Sanders Peirce may be new to some readers of this book, but we hope not to the majority. To those who know of Peirce, his story and legacy are well known and widely read, studied, and debated. One can find his intellectual disciples working in the fields of philosophy, mathematics, cosmology, philosophy, logic, computer science, and educational psychology, to name but a few. However, unlike some of his contemporaries, he's not widely known to the general public, yet his life story is fascinating and strange. With his idiosyncrasies and foibles, his twisted and melodramatic personal relationships, with enough heroes, villains, and charlatans to fill a Dickens' novel, it's a wonder more people don't know about Peirce. Without knowing that it's all true, someone reading his biography might accuse the authors of embellishment, but what comes through as you read the life story of this strange and brilliant man is the sense of his intellect and passion.

Again, it's not our intent to present a biography of Peirce; for those reading this book who are not familiar with him, there are two excellent biographies currently in print, *Charles Sanders Peirce: A Life* by Joseph Brent and a biography by Kenneth Lane Ketner, of which *His Glassy Essence: An Autobiography of Charles S. Peirce* is the first in a proposed four-volume series. I would recommend beginning with the Brent biography and once hooked on his story proceed to Ketner's more untraditional biography.

Not only is it not our intent to present a Peirce biography, it is also not our intent to prove or disprove any of the theories that Peirce put forth in his lifetime. Primarily, the intent of this book is to introduce you to a practical application of Peirce's work that has been patented and implemented within the realm of computer data structures. And in doing so, we will attempt to explain the potential implications that this practical application of Peirce's theories has to other fields of endeavor and other areas of science and philosophy.

The Practical Peirce

It's not often that one sees the words "Peirce" and "practical" in such close proximity. While Peirce is often referred to as "one of the most original minds of the later nineteenth century, and certainly the greatest American thinker ever,"[4] even his most devout supporters may find it difficult to pair these two words. It's not that people don't see the potential of his writings and life's work; it's that to date much of his legacy has come from his ideas that have generated ideas in others—from American educator and philosopher John Dewey to E. F. Codd, the inventor of the relational database. It's questionable whether those who have been influenced by Peirce would use the word "practical" when speaking of his work. So, one of the goals of this book is to introduce you to the Triadic Continuum and attempt to explain how this model has been used to invent a *practical* computer data structure, not only more powerful than any presently in use, but with implications far beyond the computer information technology realm. That seems like quite a tall order for the two of us who are not considered Peirce scholars; but it's often true that the most unique views of thought come from an outsider's point of view.

As I mentioned above, the main goal of this book is to introduce you to the Triadic Continuum and its implications in other areas of study. But, before I do, there are two other topics I'd like to cover that have an important impact on how you'll accept the premise we set forth in the last chapter of the book. So let's begin with the first of two topics pertaining to Peirce.

Peirce the Scientist

As some others do, Mazzagatti believes that Peirce was primarily a scientist and not primarily a philosopher and logician. You may be thinking that anyone who knows of Peirce knows that he was a scientist, but as Max Fisch, an early Peirce scholar noted

> It is not sufficiently recognized that Peirce's career was that of a scientist, not a philosopher; and that during his lifetime he was known and valued chiefly as a scientist, only secondarily as a logician, and scarcely at all as a philosopher. Even his work in philosophy and logic will not be understood until this fact becomes a standing premise of Peircian studies.[5]

More recently, Peirce biographer Kenneth Ketner has explained to me that he has "personally been arguing for some time that Peirce was a physicist who like Einstein also considered philosophical topics. The perceived view is that he was a philosopher who dabbled in physics."[6]

It is well known that Peirce spent 30 years with the Coast and Geodetic Survey of the United States,[7] a predecessor of the present day National Oceanic and Atmospheric Administration (NOAA),[8] conducting research in Geodesy, "the science of measuring and monitoring the size and shape of the Earth and the location of points on its surface"[9] and in the measurement of gravity. While conducting research in astronomy, Peirce produced his only published book, a monograph entitled *Photometric Research*, which was "Peirce's major contribution to astronomy."[10]

Let me say again that it's not that he is not recognized as a scientist; it is however that not enough recognition has been given to the fact that he was a scientist foremost and a philosopher as a result of his inclinations and interests. By no means do I mean to take away from his accomplishments in philosophy, logic, linguistics, and sign theory, or that he wasn't a philosopher or logician. But, one of our underlying premises is that Peirce looked at the world's phenomenon and the phenomena of the mind not primarily as a man of pure thought might, but with his feet firmly planted in science, using the same methodologies, analytical thought processes, and strategies in attempting to explain philosophical ideas as he used in the sciences.

In an essay by Peirce scholar Carolyn Eisele, she states "Peirce frequently asserted that he was reared in the laboratory. His father, Benjamin Peirce was professor of mathematics and natural philosophy at Harvard University at the time of Charles' birth; he personally supervised his son's early education and inculcated in him an analytic and scientific mode of thought."[11] Peirce admits it himself when he writes that

> I had been in training in the chemical laboratory. I was thoroughly grounded not only in all that was then known of physics and chemistry, but also in the way in which those who were successfully advancing knowledge proceeded. I have paid the most attention to the methods of the most exact sciences, have intimately communed with some of the greatest minds of our times in physical science, and have myself made positive contributions—none of them of any very great importance, perhaps—in mathematics, gravitation, optics, chemistry, astronomy, etc. I am saturated, through and through, with the spirit of the physical sciences.[12]

Peirce also acknowledges that he is primarily a scientist when he writes "... I belong to the guild of science, have learned one of its trades and am saturated with its current notions."[13]

As a member of this guild of scientists, Peirce developed "his theory of conformal map projections"[14] that resulted in his invention of the Quincuncial Projection Map of the Earth. As a member, he was the "first to relate the length of the meter to the wavelength of light."[15] He also "investigated the form of the galactic cluster in which the sun is situated."[16] And some believe that he may have "invented electrical computing"[17] through his pioneer work and belief that logical operations could be accomplished through the use of electrical switching circuits.

As with most conscientious scientists, Peirce kept abreast of past and present research and trends in science as can be seen in the following review of 18th century British Empiricist George Berkeley's essay on cognitive theory.

> Berkeley's theory of vision was an important step in the development of the associationalist psychology. He thought all our conceptions of body and of space were simply reproductions in the imagination of sensations of touch (including the muscular sense). This, if it were true, would be a most surprising case of mental chemistry, that is of a sensation being felt and yet so mixed with others that we cannot by an act of simple attention recognize it. Doubtless this theory had its influence in the production of Hartley's system.[18]

In mathematics, Peirce scholar Eisele has organized Peirce's ideas in her four-volume work *The New Elements of Mathematics by Charles S. Peirce*. As she says in the opening of volume one, "But Peirce's widely diversified researches as a pure mathematician have yet to be understood, yet to be assessed, yet to be related to the developments in mathematics of his own lifetime."[19]

And finally, Peirce signed a contract with publisher Putnam's Sons in 1896 to write a volume on the history of science; but, as with many of the pressing responsibilities in his life, "that commitment was never realized."[20] In 1916, Putnam's wrote to an inquirer "Mr. Charles S. Peirce planned to write a history of science, and it was announced by our house some time ago, but it was never published, as Mr. Peirce died before its completion."[21]

While it may seem obvious that Peirce thought of himself as a scientist, it is also obvious that much of his work is in logic and philosophy. But, it also appears that Peirce was well aware of the estrangement between the scientist and the philosopher, between the thinker and the experimenter. Writing about pragmatism, Peirce addresses the dichotomy that he perceives between the scientist and the philosopher when he says about himself

The writer of this article has been led by much experience to believe that every physicist, and every chemist, and, in short, every master in any department of experimental science, has had his mind moulded by his life in the laboratory to a degree that is little suspected. The experimentalist himself can hardly be fully aware of it, for the reason that the men whose intellects he really knows about are much like himself in this respect.[22]

That laboratory life did not prevent the writer (who here and in what follows simply exemplifies the experimentalist type) from becoming interested in methods of thinking; and when he came to read metaphysics, although much of it seemed to him loosely reasoned and determined by accidental prepossessions, yet in the writings of some philosophers, especially Kant, Berkeley, and Spinoza, he sometimes came upon strains of thought that recalled the ways of thinking of the laboratory, so that he felt he might trust to them; all of which has been true of other laboratory-men.[23]

The Scientist Philosopher

And, so it seems that Peirce was fully aware of the influence of his scientific nature, experience, and methods on his attempts to fathom the deep mysteries that underlie much of philosophy. As he says to Paul Carus, "editor of the Monist, 'Few philosophers, if any have gone to their work as well equipped as I, in the study of other systems and in the various branches of science,'"[24]

We hear him speak again of the difference between the philosopher (metaphysician) and the scientist in a review of Josiah Royce's *The World and the Individual*. In this passage Peirce begins with the philosopher

All that his sort of reasoning, therefore, has to do is to develop a preconceived idea; and it never reaches any conclusion at all as to what is or is not true of the world of existences. The metaphysician, on the other hand, is engaged in the investigation of matters of fact, and the only way to matters of fact is the way of experience. The only essential difference between metaphysics and meteorology, linguistics, or chemistry, is that it does not avail itself of microscopes, telescopes, voyages, or other means of acquiring recondite experiences, but contents itself with ascertaining all that can be ascertained from such experience as every man undergoes every day and hour of his life. All other differences between philosophy and the special sciences are mere consequences of this one.[25]

Over and over he makes the point that one needs to use more than human experience—the philosopher's method—to understand and make sense of the perceived phenomena of the world, that one needs to use formal trial and error experimentation. As when he writes

> I am very far from holding that experience is our only light; Whewell's views of scientific method seem to me truer than Mill's; so much so that I should pronounce the known principles of physics to be but a development of original instinctive beliefs. Yet I cannot help acknowledging that the whole history of thought shows that our instinctive beliefs, in their original condition, are so mixed up with error that they can never be trusted till they have been corrected by experiment.[26]

While it may be obvious, Peirce thought of himself as a scientist and conducted his work not only through thought but also through observation and scientific experimentation. But, where does this leave us? What does this mean to the main goal of this book, which is to introduce you to a practical application of Peirce's work? Well, for one thing, understanding these two points helps to lay the foundation to understand Mazzagatti's belief that Peirce did all of the work of his lifetime with his feet firmly planted in the world of science, and that his work in signs, existential graphs, logic, and even in philosophy all stemmed from his lifelong attempt to prove and communicate a much grander scientific theory with philosophical overtones.

Peirce's Grand Theory

So what is this grand theory? Simply stated, Mazzagatti believes that it is possible that Peirce saw in his mind's eye a structure that was composed of a continuum of triads, organized in a repeating hierarchy and connected in a simple, elegant, and yet very specific way. And she believes that he may have made the connection that this structure is a model of the physical architecture of the human brain and that it holds the key to how brain functions and reasoning occurs. She also believes that from the moment he saw this structure until his death, all of his years of work were in support of his attempt, sometimes successfully and at other times unsuccessfully, to explain and communicate this structure in the rigorous manner of a scientist. In the rest of this chapter I hope to shed some light onto why Mazzagatti believes this is so. I'll do this by examining five of Peirce's most well known areas of thought: his attempt to systematically organize knowledge, his theory of signs, his logic of relatives, existential graphs, and his interpretation of three methods of reasoning: induction, deduction, and abduction.

I need to preface the following discussion by saying that it isn't my intention to present an in-depth explanation of each of these accomplishments and their implications to science or philosophy—a quick Google search will identify dozens of books, papers, Web pages, and doctoral dissertations that do that—however, it is necessary for me to briefly, and I'm sure to some readers quite superficially, highlight each of these accomplishments in order to explain why Mazzagatti believes they support her ideas.

On A New List of Categories

Mazzagatti believes that while Peirce was conducting traditional metaphysical investigations on the nature of how knowledge is systematically organized—investigating matters of fact by way of experience—that he may have conceived of a structure and its mechanism that could scientifically account for how humans reason. Mazzagatti believes that this happened very early in his life. By his mid to late 20s, Peirce was attempting to develop a philosophical and intellectual theory to classify knowledge. It appears to have been a preoccupation, and even obsession, as indicated in a letter to Italian philosopher Mario Calderoni

> It was in the desperate endeavor to make a beginning of penetrating into that riddle that on May 14, 1867, after three years of almost insanely concentrated thought, hardly interrupted even by sleep, I produced my one contribution to philosophy in the "New List of Categories" ... [27]

In the above quote, Peirce refers to his article, "On a New List of Categories" published in the *Proceedings of the American Academy of Arts and Sciences* in 1868. While many see this paper as solely the beginning of Peirce's outline for his pragmatic philosophy, if one looks at his ensuing work in the years between 1867 and when this letter to Calderoni was written in 1905, Mazzagatti believes that it isn't difficult to imagine that when he refers to "riddle," he may be referring, not only to the mystery of human existence and the relation to God and Nature, but also to the mystery of reasoning and thought.[28]

Mazzagatti believes that it was sometime during this period that Peirce may have had a glimmer of the structure that Mazzagatti later called the Triadic Continuum, for it was also in this paper that we see Peirce's "earliest attempt at an account of signs."[29]

Theory of Signs

One of Peirce's most well known theories is also elucidated within the paper "On a New List of Categories." Within this paper we find Peirce's "earliest significant attempt at an account of signs."[30] His Theory of Signs, "semiotics (also spelled semeiotics) is the study of signs and sign systems. This includes the investigation of apprehension, prediction, and meaning: how it is that we develop meaning, make predictions, and apprehend the world."[31] Mazzagatti believes that after envisioning in his mind's eye the structure of the brain, he was searching for ways to explain what he saw. What tools did he have at the time for explaining what he saw? Not more than words and mathematics, Mazzagatti conjectures. So, he began by forming a model of what he saw in words and these words took the form of his theory of signs. As he tells Calderoni in the same letter from 1905, "All of our thoughts of every description are signs."[32]

Others have remarked, "The importance of semiotics for Peirce was wide ranging"[33] without necessarily catching its full import. Peirce himself said

> it has never been in my power to study anything—mathematics, ethics, metaphysics, gravitation, thermodynamics, optics, chemistry, comparative anatomy, astronomy, psychology, phonetics, economics, the history of science, whist, men and women, wine, metrology, except as a study of semeiotic[34]

He not only saw everything as the study of signs, "he is keen to associate signs with cognition. In particular, he claims that all thought is in signs...."[35] He called them 'thought-signs. And, as he explained thought-signs, he relied on the concept of the "triad," which would predominate his writings. "Now a sign has, as such, three references: first, it is a sign **to** some thought which interprets it; second, it is a sign **for** some object to which in that thought it is equivalent; third, it is a sign, **in** some respect or quality, which brings it into connection with its object."[36] (Emphasis Peirce's) As anyone who knows Peirce will immediately understand, the concept of the triad is extremely important to him; some would say almost obsessively so—but, and as you will see in later chapters, for good reason. Mazzagatti's Triadic Continuum is composed of simple triads that she believes Peirce saw. Mazzagatti believes that his theory of signs was not only important to him as a way to explain how thought occurs, but also is a direct result of his seeing the structure and how it is organized and connected.

Over the course of his future writings he continuously re-explains what he means by his theory of signs, inventing words and new theories to capture the meaning that he knows conclusively. As Mazzagatti says, "There are no ifs in Peirce's writings;"[37] he intuitively understands what he has discovered and he is simply trying to define what he knows is true. As he matures intellectually, he redefines his terms, modifies his ideas, and even develops new theories. For example, in a letter to his former student Christine Ladd-Franklin, Peirce emphasized that "pragmatism is one of the results of my study of the formal laws of signs, a study guided by mathematics and by the familiar facts of everyday experience and by no other science whatever."[38] To Mazzagatti, there is never any question about what he sees at the heart of his theory—he is simply trying to scientifically connect the dots for his reader.

Also, while reading Peirce, it sometimes seems that there is an overlap between scientist and metaphysician. While reading the different explanations of his theory of signs he seems to mix the metaphysical with the scientific, in a creative rush to bring scientific rigor to matters that might at first blush seem to be metaphysical. It must have been incredibly exhilarating to understand the structure and mechanism of how we reason, but also incredibly frustrating to be unable to completely articulate it to others.

Before continuing, let me summarize our thesis to this point. It is Mazzagatti's theory that early in his life, while conducting thought experiments on how knowledge is categorized, that Peirce either had one of those "Eureka Moments"—instantly grasping a new idea—or possibly that he may have grappled with the idea until it became clear. But, however it happened, that Peirce invented his theory of signs as his way to describe a structure and a process of how experience and meaning are recorded, memories constructed, and previously stored knowledge accessed.

The Logic of Relatives

Another possible fallout of his vision is Peirce's work on the logic of relatives. As is described in Chapters 7, 8 and 9, Peirce was fascinated with categories, associations, and relations. Maybe it wasn't a conscious fascination, as cognitive psychologists have suggested, "we think with the aid of categories."[39] And it is well established that some people think more categorically than others. If we assume that Peirce was a highly categorical, logical, and mathematical thinker, we can see how another area of his work might have been developed as a way to convey his theories on cognition and the brain. In 1870 Peirce contributed a paper that appeared as an addendum to a chapter in *Studies in Logic of the Johns Hopkins University*.[40] Here he began to write about relations in logical and semiotic aspects, "as distinguished from, though closely coordinated with, their more properly formal, mathematical, or objective aspects."[41] Mazzagatti believes that this is another example of Peirce continuing intellectual growth as he thinks more deeply about his underlying theory of reasoning. As I'll explain more in later chapters, Mazzagatti adamantly believes that Peirce knew that everything is in the structure and everything comes out of the structure. That may sound like intellectual hubris, but allow us some latitude until you understand Mazzagatti's reinterpretation of Peirce's theory as explained in later chapters.

For now, it is only important to understand that Mazzagatti believes that Peirce's intellectual development of the concepts of logical relatives fits into his growing knowledge of the implications of his underlying theory. Put another way, the more he thought about the underlying structure, the more he learned and understood the theory, but he also uncovered new ways to look at old problems and ideas.

Existential Graphs

As Peirce continued to analyze and consider the implications of his theory of signs, and its relationship to reasoning, he may have felt unable to accurately portray what he saw in his own mind. With background, experience, and interests touching almost all of the sciences and technologies in use in the second half of the 19th century, he must have been drawn to a more visual and diagrammatic method to analyze his theories. In the early 1880s Peirce invented several different methods to show the relationship of signs. One of these visualization methods was called diagrammatic reasoning, which was a method he used to visualize reasoning by constructing a diagram on which he was able to perform "experiments," take note of their results, assure himself that the results of the experiment could be replicated, and be able to express the results in general terms. As he says, "This was a discovery of no little importance, showing, as it does, that all knowledge without exception comes from observation."[42] While finding these types of visualization somewhat enlightening, "his early graphs couldn't express all possible combinations of Boolean operators, quantifiers, and their scope."[43] He later developed a method that he found more suited to showing relationships called "Existential Graphs."

Existential graphs were tools Peirce "invented as a means of diagrammatic logical analysis."[44] He used them to visually and diagrammatically represent logical relationships. One author calls them "a curious offspring of the marriage of Peirce the logician/mathematician with Peirce the founder of a major strand of semiotics."[45] By "curious marriage," the author really hits the nail on the head—Peirce the founder of the theory of signs used his skills of the thinker and scientist to develop a way to explain his theories. But what was Peirce really trying to visualize? As he writes himself in an explanation of existential graphs

> Thus the system of existential graphs is a rough and generalized diagram of the Mind, and it gives a better idea of what the mind is, from the point of view of logic, than could be conveyed by any abstract account of it.[46]

While the prevailing view is that these graphs are tools to analyze logical reasoning and show relationships, Mazzagatti believes that they may have had a different use as well. In Chapter 4, I explain how Mazzagatti visualizes the Triadic Continuum—how it's composed of nodes and connexions, or as Peirce often called them, "spots" and "connexions" or "ligatures," respectively—and how the form and structure of the Triadic Continuum dictates its function. I'll also explain in a later chapter that Mazzagatti developed her own visualization technique so that she could show the power of the structure to others, and so that she was able to see the extent of its power herself. As she explains, her visualization technique, which took its inspiration and form from her 35 years of work in the field of computer data structures, became her way to visualize the interconnectedness of the relations in the Triadic Continuum. Likewise, she believes that Peirce may have developed the Existential Graphs as more than a philosophical, or even mathematical tool, but as a way for him to visualize reasoning and thought, as a scientist would develop techniques and methods by which he could test his theories. This might be what he was referring to when he wrote

> Accordingly, when I say that Existential Graphs put before us moving pictures of thought, I mean of thought in its essence.[47]

While Peirce was not always accepted by the academic community, nevertheless, he corresponded with many other scientists, mathematicians, and philosophers, was thoroughly well-read and involved with the most cutting edge science of his day. It is therefore safe to assume that he was most likely aware of the tools and techniques that were currently available in the late 19th century and realized that there weren't any that were up to the task; so he must have had to develop his own tools to visualize the relationships inherent in whatever structure he envisioned. As well, it is apparent from the following that he knew that Existential Graphs were not perfect

> I trust by this time, Reader, that you are conscious of having some idea, which perhaps is not so dim as it seems to you to be, of what I mean by calling Existential Graphs a moving-picture of Thought. Please note that I have not called it a perfect picture. I am aware that it is not so: indeed, that is quite obvious. But I hold that it is considerably more nearly perfect than it seems to be at first glance, and quite sufficiently so to be called a portraiture of Thought.[48]

Mazzagatti suggests that it would take the advent of computers, the invention of complex data structures and data visualization tools before the necessary knowledge and techniques were available to create a "more nearly perfect" way to visualize how thought is recorded and accessed. And, she believes that the combination of the structure she discovered and emerging knowledge representation software tools, such as those developed to visualize conceptual structures may be used together to actually visualize a moving picture of thought.[49]

Induction, Deduction, and Abduction

The last theme that I want to talk about in support of Mazzagatti's belief that throughout his life Peirce was directed toward supporting and communicating his theory of reasoning is his 50-year discussion of induction, deduction, and abduction as methods of reasoning. Peirce writes that

> I have always, since early in the sixties, recognized three different types of reasoning, viz: 1st, Deduction which depends on our confidence in our ability to analyze the meanings of the signs in or by which we think; 2nd, Induction, which depends upon our confidence that a run of one kind of experience will not be changed or cease without some indication before it ceases; and 3rd, Retroduction, or Hypothetic Inference, which depends on our hope, sooner or later, to guess at the conditions under which a given kind of phenomenon will present itself interpretation of three methods of reasoning: induction, deduction, and abduction.[50]

Peirce used the word "retroduction" and "abduction" interchangeably to mean a cognitive process "with which we engender new ideas."[51] Some would say

> one of Peirce's most original contributions ... was the discovery that besides the traditional methods of inference, deduction and induction, there is a third method, or better a *first* method, which he called *abduction* or *retroduction*.

> It is abduction which introduces innovation, which starting from facts, broadens our knowledge by means of explanatory theories. Abduction is not merely a "logical operation," but it is rather ... that spontaneous activity of the mind which makes the strange familiar, making sense of what has surprised us.[52]

In the last chapter of this book I briefly talk about the research Mazzagatti and her colleagues are conducting to identify the mechanisms and strategies that underlie how her invention processes information, using a series of "algorithmic thinking strategies." Mazzagatti believes that it may be possible to extrapolate her results from the context of her computer implemented Triadic Continuum, to the thinking strategies of the human brain. I mention this because it is important to understand that Mazzagatti has confidence that, put another way, Peirce's discussion of induction, deduction, and abduction was another attempt at defining what he believed were the three main thinking strategies. Mazzagatti believes there are more than three strategies, but for now it is important only to recognize that Peirce may have been using these three to explain the thinking strategies of human behavior. It is also interesting to notice that he expressed his theories of induction, deduction, and abduction in the venue of scientific methodology. As the editors of *The Collected Papers of Charles Sander Peirce* note in their introduction to Volume 2, published in 1932

> The aspect of logic which seems to have interested him longest and most deeply, and which makes his studies significant even today, is scientific methodology, particularly the logic of discovery. This includes his development of the "frequency theory" of probability, his original theory of abduction, or the method of obtaining new ideas, and his novel treatment of induction which is shown to be closely related to the other two methods.[53]

Returning to an earlier point, we believe that it was nearly impossible for Peirce to think in a manner other than that of a scientist. So it seems fitting that he talks about these three kinds of reasoning in the context of the reasoning methodology for which he himself worked and thought most comfortably—the scientific method.

Why Not Just Say It?

I've often listened to Mazzagatti explain her belief that throughout his life, Peirce's work was directed toward supporting and communicating his theory of reasoning. Being a straightforward person, I've found myself thinking, "So why didn't he just come out and say that all of his theories were directed toward explaining the structure that Mazzagatti believes he saw?" After ten years of reading about him, reading his own writings, reading how others explain his work, and interviewing Mazzagatti, I think I've answered my own question. I think there are three possible explanations.

The first deals with Peirce's use of terms and the context within which he uses them. As I've tried to make clear, Peirce was a scientist with a philosophical bent. He was also, as many have labeled him, a polymath. His interests, experiences, and education were highly diverse and extensive. And, his vocations and avocations all had complex sets of terms and language to govern discourse on their subject matter—physics, mathematics, philosophy, all of these with their own arcane terminology—some shared terms different only in a slight nuance of meaning. Take for example Peirce's use of the word "valencies." In his writings he uses this term as a chemist would, when he says "that every element has a fixed number of loose ends,"[54] He uses it to mean something similar, but within a different context, when he talks about the elements of the Phaneron, which is his name for the structure and contents (experiences, memories, imagination, thought, mind, habit, etc.) of the human brain. In a discussion of the Phaneron he hints that valencies govern the composition of its structure.[55] There are numerous other examples in his writing where shared terminology, which to him may have seemed natural and clear, makes most readers pause, stop, and ponder in which context he's writing. It makes for a difficult trek through his writing.

Second, after reading Peirce in his own words, I believe that he may have thought that he had, in fact, stated that reasoning is due to the structural organization of thought-signs. Let me tell you why I believe that. After writing some of the patents associated with Mazzagatti's Triadic Continuum, and spending a week digesting the two main patents (U.S. Patent numbers 6,961,733 and 7,158,975), I feel that I now have a good grasp on the structure of the Triadic Continuum, what the invention is about, and what it can do. That said, after doing all of that, when I go back and reread passages of Peirce, I'm struck with how clear the meaning of his words really are. Some readers of Peirce find his writing obtuse, as I did in the beginning. However, with a firm understanding of Mazzagatti's structure, you find yourself exclaiming aloud that you can see what he's talking about. For example, after learning about the structure of the Triadic Continuum, I went back and reread Peirce's definition of the Phaneron and valencies, only to find it a complete vindication of Mazzagatti's premise that the scientist Peirce saw the structure of reasoning, as a physical entity.

When Mazzagatti, her colleagues, and I talk about understanding Peirce we often use the metaphor of peeling an onion—there are so many layers of understanding. At one level you may read him and understand that he is talking about reasoning in a very philosophical way, and then after you understand the Triadic Continuum you find yourself able to peel back another layer and hear that he is talking about human reasoning in a very scientific way. Mazzagatti often says that people assume that Peirce is theorizing (about the method of reasoning), but with an understanding of the structure of the Triadic Continuum, she knows that he's not guessing, he actually saw the structure. For now, you're going to have to trust us on this. Our argument holds water only if after finishing this book, understanding the Triadic Continuum, and rereading Peirce (in a new context), you understand that to the best of his ability, Peirce was saying that he saw a structure of thought and reasoning.

The third possible explanation that helps me answer my question is that there may still exist proof of the structure, proof that may exist as diagrams within manuscripts that are not readily available. As the Peirce Edition Project, a center for research related to Peirce's work, states

> More than 80,000 manuscript pages make up the Harvard Peirce Papers, a collection which includes the vast majority of publishable materials in the Peirce canon.
>
> If all of Peirce's writings were to be published, they would fill over 100 volumes."[56]

While much of Peirce's writing is available in collected forms, all is not. Mazzagatti and I have spoken with people who know of manuscripts that only a few Peirce scholars have seen, but are not easily available to everyone without trips to Harvard, Indiana University, or Texas Tech. This isn't anyone's fault; a cadre of dedicated Peirce scholars has been working for years to make his writings available. It's simply that Peirce was known to make diagrams and it seems easier to obtain his writings than his drawings. Mazzagatti and I continue to believe that there are manuscript pages, notebook entries, and possibly scratch pages with diagrams that no one has yet been able to decipher. Besides this possibility is also that of the unfortunate treatment of some of his papers after Peirce's death. Peirce biographer Joseph Brent mentions that when Paul Weiss, one of the first editors of Peirce's collected writings, began the task of organizing Peirce's manuscripts "he discovered in a basket marked 'to be discarded' one of Peirce's most important papers in logic"[57] Might other manuscripts have already been discarded? With the sheer quantity of papers, the number of people involved, and the length of years gone by, it isn't impossible to think that some have been permanently misplaced or destroyed.

One surviving example of a diagram of interest to Mazzagatti comes from a Peirce manuscript page. Later, in Chapter 4 you'll see what Mazzagatti's Triadic Continuum looks like—she believes that the following diagram [58] is an example of how Peirce drew the same triadic structure as Mazzagatti.

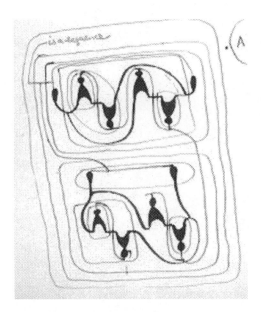

Figure 1–1

To summarize Mazzagatti's theory, she believes that a youthful Charles Peirce, while conducting thought experiments on how knowledge is categorized, conceived of a tremendously broad and audacious idea, that of a structure that models the structure of the human brain as well as models how it functions to reason. That he conceived of his theory of signs, logic of relative, existential graphs, and his explanation of induction, deduction, and especially abduction as ways to describe this structure and the process of how experience and meaning are recorded, memories constructed, and previously stored knowledge accessed. And, that the remainder of his life was his attempt, as a scientist to elucidate and communicate this grand theory to other scientists and philosophers.

2

The Rediscovery of the Triadic Continuum

No perfect continuum can be defined by a [asymmetrical] dyadic relation ... But if we take instead a triadic relation ... to fix our ideas, that ... it is quite evident that a continuum will result like a self-returning line with no discontinuity whatever ...
Charles Sanders Peirce[1]

As described in the last chapter, Charles Sanders Peirce's underlying goal, his life's quest, was to discover and explain how we reason. He tackled this problem not simply as a philosopher, fashioning theory out of mental reflection, but as a mathematician and scientist, whose research was geared toward uncovering the secret of the process and structure of reasoning. Semiotics, or the theory of signs, was his attempt to describe a process and a structure to explain how meaning is transmitted and understood, or in other words—how we reason.

When Jane Campbell Mazzagatti conceived of the structure of the Triadic Continuum, she wasn't trying to explain the workings of the human brain; she was working on a project directed at developing a new type of computer data structure. At the time, Mazzagatti was employed by Unisys Corporation, a company with roots going back to the development of ENIAC and UNIVAC, the earliest all-electronic business and scientific computers. She and her colleagues were involved in a research and development project with the goal of creating a computer program to surpass conventional databases and change how large amounts of information are collected, stored, and queried.

Mazzagatti's colleagues were made up of a number of Unisys engineers and a small group of researchers from an outside company. These outside researchers had introduced the Unisys team to Peirce through the writings of their late chief scientist Eugene "Gene" Pendergraft. Pendergraft was introduced to Peirce while reading John Dewey's book *Logic: The Theory of Inquiry* while stationed in the South Pacific during World War II. Those who knew Pendergraft talk about the influence this book had on him. A colleague, with whom he worked and corresponded for many years, until Pendergraft's death in 1997, says that Gene carried Dewey's book around with him everywhere.

> He carried this around with him from island to island as they island hopped in the Pacific theater during World War II. He said that when not flying, he tried to forget about the war—since he was in a squadron where the turnover was quite high. He was one of the few that made it through the whole tour of duty. He said he would take this book down to the beach and just sit there and read and try to get into philosophy and put all this other stuff out of his head. So, at this time he was motivated to think deeply about things that he might not have at other times. I think Gene was profoundly influenced by Dewey and ultimately came to understand Peirce and the whole Pragmatic philosophical system. [2]

To fully understand the connection between Peirce's theories and Mazzagatti's Triadic Continuum, it is helpful to understand how these ideas and references stimulated Pendergraft; these ideas would excite and stimulate him for the rest of his life.

First, it was within Dewey's *Logic* that Pendergraft was introduced to the idea that logical thinking is determined operationally, that is that the process of inquiry is a biological operation initiated through the senses. In Dewey's words:

> It is obvious without argument that when men inquire they employ their eyes and ears, their hands and their brains. These organs, sensory, motor, or central, are biological. Hence, although biological operations and structures are not sufficient conditions of inquiry, they are necessary conditions.[3]

Dewey, who was a student of Peirce's at Johns Hopkins, was influenced by Peirce and proposed in *Logic* that inquiry is the mechanism of human thought, and gives Peirce credit for first understanding "the principle of the continuum of inquiry."[4] Dewey also mentions his indebtedness to Peirce as the "first writer on logic to make inquiry and its methods the primary and ultimate source of logical subject matter."[5]

Second, Dewey argued that we interact with our "world through self-guided activity that coordinates and integrates sensory and motor responses."[6] The implication for how we understand and gain knowledge is clear: "the world is not passively perceived and thereby known; active manipulation of the environment is involved integrally in the process of learning from the start."[7] Dewey believed, and Pendergraft came to believe, that philosophers "had drawn too stark a distinction between thought, the domain of knowledge, and the world of fact to which thought purportedly referred," believing that thought existed apart from the world.[8]

And finally, it was within *Logic* that Pendergraft was introduced to *The Collected Works of Charles Sanders Peirce*, a collection of Peirce's writings thematically organized. First published in 1931, these six volumes contain a portion of Peirce's manuscripts and articles arranged by topic.

It's not hard to imagine that Pendergraft was intellectually stimulated by the notion that thinking, reasoning, and learning are based on biological structures that function through a series of physical operations. After the war, Pendergraft attended the University of Texas, and received degrees in both mathematics and philosophy. He went on to develop his own theories on mechanized learning and, based on his understanding of Peirce—Pendergraft theorized that machines, specifically computers, could be made to learn like a living brain.

One of his first experiences putting theory into practice was an attempt to develop computerized language translation. In the early 1960s, Pendergraft co-directed a project at the University of Texas at Austin to use computers to translate German, Russian, Japanese, and Chinese into English.[9] His theories on mechanical translation were based on his interpretation of Peirce's ideas. While he knew that he was searching for some type of new data structure, he also understood that instantaneous translation required a structure to reside in computer memory. However, computer memory at the time was too small to allow this. While he and his team were able to demonstrate a rudimentary form of mechanical translation, the project was halted when U.S. Air Force officials cancelled funding. With this setback, Pendergraft put his ideas of mechanized learning on hold until computer technology caught up to his prophetic thinking.

In the early 1990s, when Pendergraft thought the time was right for mechanized learning, he and a small group of programmers and entrepreneurs formed

Autognomics Corporation. It was immediately evident to the founders that a project of this magnitude would be too costly for a small startup company, so they decided to pursue a financial and technical relationship with a larger company. The companies they contacted were IBM, HP (Hewlett-Packard), DEC (Digital Equipment Corporation, now part of Hewlett-Packard,) Sun Microsystems, and Unisys Corporation. Of these, only Unisys Corporation and HP responded to their inquiry.[9]

HP soon dropped out of negotiations and after a series of interviews and discussions about Pendergraft's theories, representatives of Unisys agreed to a limited research and development relationship. A combined Unisys and Autognomics team was formed with the Unisys team located in Malvern, Pennsylvania and the Autognomics team situated throughout the North Eastern U.S. Their task was to design and code a software data structure to enable mechanized learning. This program was code-named "Autognome," from the Greek "auto" or self and "gnome" meaning intelligence or as the Autognomics folks defined it, a "self-knowing" machine.[10]

People joining the team began by reviewing two documents that Pendergraft had written to explain his theories. The first document was a design specification that Pendergraft had written in 1994. This specification, which was intended to be a technical blueprint to explain the Autognome, was a combination of mathematics and computer programming descriptions based on his interpretation of Peirce's theories.[11] This blueprint and an esoteric philosophical paper, entitled *The Future's Voice: Intelligence Based on Pragmatic Logic* that Pendergraft had compiled in 1993, were required reading for those who wanted to understand Pendergraft's theories on mechanized learning.[12] However, two things stood in the way of a clear understanding of his ideas.

First, *The Future's Voice* was a conglomeration of scientific theories, philosophy, social theory, and opinion. It was so difficult to separate theory from opinion and Pendergraft from Peirce that only the bravest and most conscientious actually finished reading more than the introduction. Second, and possibly the most problematic, was Pendergraft's untimely death just as the project began. Without Pendergraft to answer practical questions, his protégé began interpreting the specification without an in-depth understanding of Peirce.

Enter Jane Campbell Mazzagatti—with an extensive background in computer hardware and software, degrees in theoretical mathematics and educational psychology, a deep personal interest in cognitive development, a non-relenting quest for knowledge, and a strong personality, Mazzagatti was the right person to judge the validity of Pendergraft's interpretation of Peirce's theories.

As she began work on the project, Mazzagatti first read Pendergraft's blueprint specification. While she was able to follow his theoretical mathematics in the blueprint, she was unsatisfied with Pendergraft's explanation of the triadic continuum and how it should be constructed. Later, she was disappointed in Pendergraft's grasp of Peirce's theories as explained in *The Future's Voice*. For one thing, she thought it was difficult to see where Peirce left off and Pendergraft began. Unlike other team members, she decided that she needed to read Peirce's own words, so she purchased a copy of *The Collected Works of Charles Sanders Peirce* on CD-ROM. Using the CD-ROM's electronic search, she searched for terms she found in Pendergraft's writings with exact matches in Peirce's writings.

During 1998 and 1999, while the team tried unsuccessfully to produce a working software application based on Pendergraft's specification, Mazzagatti compared how Peirce defined terms with how Pendergraft interpreted the same terms. As she delved deeper into the comparison, Mazzagatti began to believe that Pendergraft and his protégé were on the wrong track.

As it became increasingly clear to team members that success wasn't eminent, many Unisys personnel requested transfers and left the team.

Meanwhile, as Mazzagatti continued to search for all the sources of information on Peirce she could locate, she became so wrapped up in Peirce's theories that she changed her doctoral thesis to a subject related to Peirce.

As she conducted research for her dissertation, Mazzagatti discovered an interesting reference to Peirce, logic, and machines in the *American Journal of Psychology*. For the inaugural issue of this journal in 1887, Peirce wrote an article in which he suggested that it should be possible to construct a machine that could reason based on logic.[13] It's important to remember that to Peirce, the concept of "logic" was equivalent to the concept of "reasoning." This paper seemed to suggest to Mazzagatti that Peirce was intimating that a machine could be constructed to reason.

As she read and learned more, Mazzagatti began to get a sense of what Peirce was envisioning when he talked about his theories of signs. And, as she filtered his ideas through her own background and experience in computer science, mathematics, and psychology, she began to see how Peirce's sign theory could be adapted to create a logical structure composed of signs that could be used in computers. And so, without the support of Pendergraft's protégé or other team members, Mazzagatti set out to design and then create a structure to store and locate information within computers.

The structure that Mazzagatti finally conceived and turned into an invention fits into the general computer category of data structures, devices for storing and locating information on computers. However, as you'll eventually come to understand, this structure is much more than that—it's a model of how we reason—a cognitive model of the brain.

3

Understanding Traditional Databases

Several existing systems permit a variety of physical representations for a given logical structure ... The complexity of the physical representations which these systems support is, perhaps, understandable, because these representations are selected in order to obtain high performance ... What is less understandable is the trend toward more and more complexity in the data structures with which ... users directly interact. Surely, in the choice of logical data structures that a system is to support, there is one consideration that is of absolutely paramount importance—and that is the convenience of the majority of users. E. F. Codd [1]

Before explaining how the computer implementation of the Triadic Continuum is constructed and used, and why it is an advancement over other computer data organization, it's important to understand a little about the strength and inherent limitations of traditional databases. This chapter contains a discussion about database structures with fairly straightforward terminology that should be common to readers with only a rudimentary understanding of how computers operate. You don't have to be a computer geek to understand my explanation, but it will help to have a basic understanding of how a computer data structure and a database work before going on to the following chapters on the construction and use of the structure known as the Triadic Continuum.

What Is a Database?

A database is simply a large collection of related data and information that can be retrieved and used. For example, the Internal Revenue Service has databases that contain related data and information about taxpayers. The last name of a taxpayer is a piece of data, a taxpayer's social security number is another piece of data, and number of exemptions associated with the taxpayer is another, and so on. In the IRS database, the data are related by the fact that it's all about taxes and taxpayers.

Before computers, data were stored on sheets of paper or on forms that were physically separated by file folders, which were often held in file cabinets. The folders and cabinet drawers were often labeled so that someone could tell at a glance what was in a drawer or a folder. The folders were probably arranged within the cabinets in some order, such as alphabetical or by date. If you visited my home and looked at how I file my old tax forms and receipts, you'd see that they're all stored in an old file cabinet, in labeled manila folders, arranged and organized by year. Continuing to use our tax example, we can think of the IRS computer as the file cabinet and the database as the set of file folders that hold all of the taxpayer information.

Data Sets

When talking about the data in a database, you may see the term "data set." A data set is a collection of related records. Using our IRS example, the following is a simple data set.

Score	William	600-00-0001	4	610-555-1234
Scoren	George	100-00-0009	2	212-555-6755
Scortia	Philomena	900-00-0003	1	215-555-8900
Scorzelli	Stephen	700-00-0007	6	512-555-0026

Figure 3–1

In the above sample data set, there are four records: one for William Score, George Scoren, Philomena Scortia, and Stephen Scorzelli. The first record, that for William Score, contains the following pieces of data: last name, "Score"; first name, "William"; Social Security Number, "600-00-0001"; number of exemptions, "4"; and telephone number, "610-555-1234."

Each record in this sample data set of four records has the same five data types, organized in columns: last name, first name, social security number, number of exemptions, and telephone number. The records in this data set are related by the fact that each record contains the same data type; not the same data, but the same type. Also, it should be obvious that a real IRS data set would contain many more data types about a taxpayer than the five shown here.

Inputting Data

Early computers used what was known as a "Hollerith Card" to hold and input data records into the computer. Also known as "punch cards," these cards were stiff pieces of cardboard that represented data by "the presence or absence of holes in pre-defined positions on the card."[2] Each punch card contained one record of a data set.

As computers became more sophisticated, punch cards were replaced as a method to input and store data with magnetic disks. However, data records, whether on punch cards or magnetic disks are simply sets of data records. It's like taking a ruled piece of paper and writing the last name, first name, social security number, number of exemptions, and telephone number of a single taxpayer on a single line. A single sheet of lined paper has about 30 lines, so if each line holds information about one taxpayer, there would be 30 taxpayers on a single sheet of paper. Finding an individual taxpayer on a single sheet of paper is pretty easy, but if we used one line for every one of the nearly 150,000,000 taxpayers in the U.S., we'd have to look through 5,000,000 sheets of paper to find any single individual. Even assuming that we only look through the pages that contain last names beginning with the letter "S," we'd still have to look through a lot of pages to find *the* William Score with the social security number we're looking for.

Before continuing, let's talk more about how data gets into a computer. In computer-speak, the term "input" refers to how data and information are received by the computer. As mentioned above, in the early days of computing, data such as our example taxpayer information was received into the computer through punch cards or magnetic disk. In more recent times, data are input into a computer through keyboard, mouse, joystick, touch screen, digital camera, scanner, or other type of electronic device. Data such as our taxpayer data, and other textual data, such as payroll data or sales transaction data for example, are generally gathered on either a paper form (e.g., insurance form) and manually entered into the computer, or entered into a computer program, which then passes the data to the database when the user presses a key or clicks a button.

However, no matter what method or device is used to input textual data records into a database, the collection of these records (or data sets) are arranged in a two-dimensional table consisting of rows and columns. The table shown below contains the data from our taxpayer database, except with rows and columns differentiated by lined borders.

Record ID	Last Name	First Name	State	Number of Exemptions	Telephone Number
110033	Score	William	Alabama	4	610-555-1234
110034	Scoren	George	Ohio	2	212-555-6755
110035	Scortia	Philomena	Pennsylvania	1	215-555-8900
110036	Scorzelli	Sandra	Montana	6	512-555-0026

Figure 3–2

As you can see, database tables contain columns and rows of data. The columns represent "categories," or a type of data value (a data type). The rows are a set of data values representing transactions or records. For example, in the table above, row 1 (Record ID 110033) is a single record set of data for one person: Last Name, Score; First Name, William; State, Alabama; Number of Exemptions, 4; and telephone number, 610-555-1234. The second column is a field named "Last Name" and it holds the last names of all of the taxpayers, such as Score, Scoren, Scortia, and Scorzelli. Notice also that I've labeled the columns with a heading to show what data is contained in the columns.

The Trouble with Tables

There are a few basic shortcomings with using tables that early database designers quickly recognized. First, the data must be searched sequentially, which means that if you're trying to locate the data for the taxpayer "Scoren, George," the computer must begin at the first data record (the first record in the table) and search through every record until a match is found for the last name of "Scoren" then for the first name "George." A problem with sequential searching is that even for a computer, it is time consuming, especially when there are hundreds of thousands or millions of records. This problem was somewhat alleviated as computers became faster and more powerful and as computer scientists designed new and faster ways to sort, index, and search large amounts of data.

The second problem, adding, changing, or deleting data and records, is actually more difficult. For example, whenever a taxpayer gets a new telephone number, changes an exemption, or needs to update some other bit of personal information, data in a record or an entire record has to be updated.

To update the data, the computer first has to locate the correct record. It does this, as explained above, by sequentially searching through the table until it finds the correct record. And while this is not a major problem, sequential searching through all records does take extra time as well as additional computer resource.

The major problem however, is not changing a single field of data in a record; it's deleting or adding a single field to the database table. When a record is deleted, say because of the death of a taxpayer, the location where the data resides in computer memory is wiped clean; the table now contains a blank record, or in other words, there's a hole in the database table. In our taxpayer example, since the data is listed sequentially (alphabetically), nothing can be written to that blank record space, unless the name of the new person to be added is the exact same as the person who was removed. Not very likely since the last name must match exactly, and the first name must fit alphabetically between the person's first name in the data record before and the first name after the record in question.

If that weren't difficult enough, when adding a new record, another problem arises. As explained above, a database is "fixed," which means that when all the original data is input, the table is written in the order in which it is received. The data might be in order by one field, such as by number or alphabetically or by multiple fields such as last name and first name. It's even possible that the data may be added in a totally random order. The problem with this is that there is no space between records for new records to be added later. Fixed tables present a problem when trying to add new information. For example, if a data record for Charlotte Scorza needed to be added to the taxpayer database, it would need to be added between the record for "Scortia" and "Scorzelli." Since there are no blank records between Scortia and Scorzelli, the new record for Charlotte Scorza can only be added at the very end of the database table. However, by doing that, the data in the table is no longer in order and whatever benefits are derived from having the data arranged sequentially, is lost by adding a record to the end of the table that should be alphabetically organized within it.

This was the state of database design in the late 1950's and early 1960's—data sets built as simple tables or arrays that were difficult to maintain and often slow to search the more data they contained.

At about this time, researchers at the RAND Corporation developed a data structure called "linked lists," which consist of a sequence of data fields with one or two pointers pointing to the next and/or previous data field.[3] These pointers, which may be at the beginning or end of each record, contain the numeric address in computer memory where the next or previous record is stored—in effect a mechanism to keep track of the next, previous, or some other sequence of data fields. For example, in our taxpayer table shown below, the pointer "110034" at the end of the record for William Score points to the memory address of the next record, which is identified with the record address "110034," which represents the record for George Scoren.

Record Address	Last Name	First Name	State	Number of Exemptions	Telephone Number	Pointer
110033	Score	William	Alabama	4	610-555-1234	110034
110034	Scoren	George	Ohio	2	212-555-6755	110035
110035	Scortia	Philomena	Pennsylvania	1	215-555-8900	110036
110036	Scorzelli	Sandra	Montana	6	512-555-0026	110037

Figure 3–3

This technique, of adding single or multiple pointers that may point forward or backward, enables the designer much more flexibility than with traditional tables. As I mentioned above, one of the major problems with tables is in the difficulty modifying data once it's in the table. Linked lists solve this by allowing the designer to add or change data in a sequence of fields without worrying about the whole data structure—as long as the pointers remain intact, the structure can be dynamically modified without losing any information or the overall organization.

The following example shows how records can be added to a linked list data structure without losing the sequential nature of the table. The following shows the same table as above with a record for Charlotte Scorza added at the end.

Record Address	Last Name	First Name	State	Number of Exemptions	Telephone Number	Pointer
110033	Score	William	Alabama	4	610-555-1234	110034
110034	Scoren	George	Ohio	2	212-555-6755	110035
110035	Scortia	Philomena	Pennsylvania	1	215-555-8900	**562031**
110036	Scorzelli	Sandra	Montana	6	512-555-0026	110037
562031	Scorza	Charlotte	Washington	0	476-555-3388	110036

Figure 3–4

When a record needs to be added, three things happen. First, the record is added to the **end** of the data structure and stored in a given memory address, in this case "562031." Next, the pointer associated with Philomena Scortia is changed from 110036 to 562031. This means that when the computer is searching for names in the structure, after reading the record for Ms. Scortia, it will immediately skip to record 562031, because that is the next "logical" record in the alphabetical list. Third, the record for Charlotte Scorza is given the pointer "110036" so that it points back to the next alphabetically organized record.

With this simple solution it doesn't matter how the records are organized, they might be next to each other or scattered throughout—all that needs to happen is that the pointer be changed to reflect where the next sequential record is located.

Pointers can also be used to delete records without actually removing the data from a linked list. All one has to do is have the pointer of the record before the record that is to be deleted point to the address of the record following the record to be deleted. For example, assume you want to delete the record containing George Scoren. All you need to do is to change the pointer for the William Score record to point to the record for Philomena Scortia as shown in Figure 3–5.

Record Address	Last Name	First Name	State	Number of Exemptions	Telephone Number	Pointer
110033	Score	William	Alabama	4	610-555-1234	**110035**
110034	Scoren	George	Ohio	2	212-555-6755	110035
110035	Scortia	Philomena	Pennsylva-nia	1	215-555-8900	110036
110036	Scorzelli	Sandra	Montana	6	512-555-0026	110037

Figure 3–5

While not a database per se, linked lists was a technique that anticipated the dynamic nature of the coming databases.

Relational Databases

While linking lists of tabular data using pointers was helpful, it still had drawbacks. For one, lists still reside in one long, somewhat sequential table of data, which is still difficult to search quickly. As well, there are issues with managing computer memory, the size of the database, and the duplication of information. However, the next advancement in databases helped alleviate some of the problems associated with long tabular lists of information.

The next major advancement was the conception of the relational database, which was proposed by British computer scientist Dr. E. F. Codd in the early 1970s. Codd, working at IBM, developed a relational database model based on mathematical set theory, which describes the properties of collections of objects. Sets can be thought of as any well-defined collection of things considered as a whole.[4] For example, a table may be considered a set of records about objects in the "real world" (e.g., taxpayer last name, first name, etc.).

A relational database can be described as a set of unordered tables from which data can be "accessed or reassembled in many different ways without having to reorganize the database tables."[5] Unordered tables mean that the data are organized in tables in such a way that the data fields are related to one another, but that the records are not ordered in any particular way. So, when a new record is added it can be conveniently added to the end of the entire table. Putting related data fields in a table and using a key to reference the set in other tables avoids duplication of data, reduces space requirements for the data set, and helps save time accessing data.

Let me explain by using the following example tables. The following table is organized by taxpayer **name** information.

Last Name	First Name	Middle Name	Honorific Prefix	Suffix	Key
Sheetz	Gail	Rose	Ms.		1
Davidson	Jeffery	M.	Mr.	Sr.	2
Mardis	Maryanne	Isabel	Dr.		3
Antonini	David	Raymond	Mr.		4

Figure 3–6

However, there might also be another table that contains taxpayer **address** information, as shown below:

Number	Apt.	Street 1	City	State	Zip Code	Key
55 W.	1278	First Ave.	Baltimore	MD	21201	1
579		Wide Rd.	Denver	CO	80030	2
875		56th St.	Bronx	NY	10453	3
410	14	North Branch	Aspen	CO	81612	4

Figure 3–7

Still, there may be other tables, with such data as taxable year, exemption, salary, or deductions, among others. The database is called "relational" for two reasons. First, because the data in each table is related about a specific category, such as all name data in a single table, it is related. Second, all the tables are related to one another through some type of master transaction table. For example, for taxable year 2006, the following master table relates all "transactions" for that year.

Name	Address	SSAN	Exemptions	Salary	Deductions
1	3	299	2	17	22
2	2	456	99	90	2389
3	9	80	45	8	78
4	88	6	2000	1	73

Figure 3–8

This master transaction table holds the index key numbers associated with the data from the appropriate table. For example, the first row in the master transaction table above holds keys for Name: key = 1; Address: key = 3; Social Security Number: key = 299; Exemptions: key = 2; Salary: key = 17; and Deductions: key = 22.

The Name column for the first record contains the index key "1" so, if we refer back to Figure 3–6, you can see that the name associated with the index key 1 is Gail Sheetz. Likewise, the index key for Address in the first record is "3," so the address for Ms. Sheetz is the address associated with index key 3, or 875 56th St. Bronx, NY 10453. And so on.

While this scheme looks complicated, it's not difficult for a computer to keep track of all the tables and the index keys, and more importantly, because the data are held in separate tables, updating and deleting data are much more efficient than single table lists, and it reduces duplication.

Some database schemes go as far as to code data in order to decrease or compress the size of the database. For example, instead of storing the 17 letters, characters, and single separating space that make up "Customer: Jackson," code "1" is stored instead. This definitely saves space in computer memory; however it introduces another table—the table used to associate the codes with the item they represent.

Another limitation of tables is that it is not easy to add or delete a single field. All records in a table are a fixed length; if a field is empty the space is wasted.

Saving Time

To save time in accessing data or to prepare data for printing, sets of indexes must be manually constructed. For example, using the data in Figure 3–6, to create an alphabetical list of the taxpayers in the database one would have to create an index that would contain the key values in alphabetical order. So, the index table would look like the following:

4
2
3
1

Figure 3–9

To access data alphabetically or to print data alphabetically, the first index key "4" locates the last name associated with that key. Looking back at Figure 3–6 you'll see that the last name associated with key "4" is Antonini; the name associated with key "2" is Davidson; with "3" is Mardis; and the name associated with key "1" is Sheetz. Or, another way to look at it is:

4	Antonini
2	Davidson
3	Mardis
1	Sheetz

Figure 3–10

Therefore, to retrieve information in alphabetical order, for a report or for some other reason entails creating an external (to the relational database) index of keys that point to data records in a specific sequence—a somewhat inefficient but necessary method for working around an inherent shortcoming.

Querying Databases

Information is typically retrieved from relational databases using specialized computer query languages. The most popular is called Structured English Query Language, which was developed by IBM computer scientists in the 1970s.[6] Called "SQL" for short, this language was designed to make getting information into and out of relational databases quicker and easier than previous methods. However, since the basic structure of a database is two-dimensional tables, SQL was designed to retrieve data from this structure, which is both its strength and weakness. The strength is that it works really well within a two-dimensional table at quickly retrieving information. Its weakness is that, while moderately easy to find answers to simple questions like, "How many exemptions does William Score have?" it's not designed to answer more complex questions like, "What is the relationship between taxpayer zip code and mean average income?" A question of this nature requires that the query software be able to identify and locate relationships that are not directly accessible from within the tabular data formatted in columns and rows. Finding answers to the more complex relationship-type questions would take the invention of structures and software a little different than relational databases using SQL.

Database Cubes

The next and last step in our discussion of the development of the database is the concept of the database cube, also known as the OLAP (on-line analytical processing) cube. First proposed by Codd in 1994, a cube can be thought of as an extension to the two-dimensional (columns and rows) table of a traditional database. In a two-dimensional table you can search and locate information about a given field in a single category. For example, you can search for the Social Security number (category) of a specific taxpayer (field).

However, cubes allow the data to be viewed in multiple dimensions and analyzed in greater detail. For example, an IRS database administrator can create a cube that can be analyzed to provide the answer to the question, "How many taxpayers, living in the 90210 zip code made over $100,000 per year in the taxable year 2005 and have 4 exemptions?"

Questions can be asked of cubes that analyze and summarize information as well as point out possible trends in the data. However, one of the main problems with cubes is that they are time-consuming to design and program. Plus, the queries are limited to the exact data in the cube at the time it is created. Therefore, every time the data in the cube changes, the cube must be recreated. This last weakness is especially bothersome if the data is transactional data that changes constantly. Say, for example, a nationwide building supply company uses database cubes to identify potential trends in their business and it takes weeks to create a cube. The data in the cube is weeks old before it is ready to query. A time lag of weeks, if not many months in some cases means that the data are outdated before the first query can be asked. Consequently, this limitation virtually eliminates the ability to perform queries in real or near-real time.

Databases Today

Just about all businesses today use relational databases to store information about customer transactions, employee records, and other historical data. Also, most companies that rely on uncovering trends in their business use database cubes. However, while being the method that most business and scientific organizations use to store and query information, these tools do have some inherent weaknesses. One such weakness, storing some types of simple ordered information, is more difficult than might be expected. For example, a simple school bus route, where a very structured and orderly roll of bus stops is difficult for a relational database, is designed to "only hold tables as unordered record lists and can retrieve an ordered list only if a specially built index is added."[7]

Other equally common tasks are facilitated by the use of databases, such as creating and building a bill of materials, which in manufacturing is a list of the product that is to be built and the components that make up the product.

> The components themselves may have components that in turn may have components and so on. A relational database table of all parts will not express the relationships of the parts to the parts of parts, and so on. These relationships express important data. To query a database for a product and all its components should be straightforward. A relational database structure makes the developer's job of answering this simple query, unnecessarily complex and difficult. Examples of this kind abound: A map and its roads, rivers, and landmarks; A web site and all its pages, links and graphics. In fact, the more complex the collection of information is, the more levels of hierarchy and cross relationships, the less possible it is to represent it within the simple table structures of a relational database.[8]

The relational database is by all accounts one of the most marvelous inventions of the 20th century, but as with most technological advances, there's always room for improvement. Even though it has its strengths, the main problem with relational databases

> is that the fundamental data structure they use is a two-dimensional table. In relational theory, data is supposed to be organized into normalized tables—that is, the data is supposed to be organized in such a way that there is only one way to get to it, allowing the developer to eliminate redundancy and ensure that changes to the data are consistent. This design technique was introduced to ensure that relational tables contained independent sets of data that were related only by a key. It derived from the mathematics of Set Theory, but the problem is that Set Theory is not capable of representing all the relationships and structures that data can have.[9]

In the above quotes the author uses the word "relationship." Relationships are very important to how databases are organized and what type of information is easily located in one. Database scientists spend a great deal of time trying to identify relationships that exist within a database and an equally large amount of time trying to create methods to locate these relationships. As you'll see as we continue, the simplicity with which relationships are uncovered and discovered within the structure of the Triadic Continuum is one if its fundamental features that makes it so much more powerful than traditional databases, relational databases, and even database cubes.

One final thought before moving on is about Codd, the late inventor of the relational database. Codd earned his PhD under Arthur Burks, who coincidentally was the editor of volumes seven and eight of "*Collected Papers of Charles Sanders Peirce.*" Peirce, who as we've already said had a foundation in mathematics, did much to broaden the use of relational algebra. "At IBM, Codd promoted relational algebra as the foundation for database systems, a version of which was adopted for the query language SQL, which is used in all relational database systems today."[10]

4

Constructing the Triadic Continuum

The precise definition is still in doubt; but Kant's definition, that a continuum is that of which every part has itself parts of the same kind, seems to be correct. In accordance with this it seems necessary to say that a continuum, where it is continuous and unbroken, contains no definite parts; that its parts are created in the act of defining them and the precise definition of them breaks the continuity. Charles Sanders Peirce[1]

In a true continuum there must be a common moment, but not an absolute instant, independent of all that is before and after. Charles Sanders Peirce[2]

After reading the last chapter, you have a basic understanding of the evolution of today's databases, how they're structured, the type of data they hold, the type of questions that they can be asked, and their strengths and weaknesses.

In this chapter I'll explain the fundamentals of the Triadic Continuum: its basic components and how its structure is constructed. In the chapter that follows this, I'll explain how information is found within the structure, how relationships are discovered, and why it's exponentially more powerful than today's databases.

The Triadic Continuum

As I've said before, we believe that it was Charles Peirce's lifetime goal to discover and explain the mechanism and structure of human reasoning; Gene Pendergraft wanted to create a self-organizing machine;[3] while Jane Mazzagatti's original interest was in building a computer data structure.[4] However, they had one thing in common; they all believed that their goal would be realized only by the discovery of a physical structure, constructed in such a way as to record and hold all of the relationships existing within a given set of data.

Peirce pursued this structure, which he called the Phaneron, through his thoughts and experiments as a scientist and mathematician. Pendergraft pursued it through his work on mechanical language translation.[5] Mazzagatti, with her background in mathematics, educational psychology, and computer science came at it from computer data structures, but all three were looking for the same structure, the structure that today, Mazzagatti calls "the Triadic Continuum," "the Phaneron," or simply "K."

The Triadic Continuum as Computer Structure

As many who have had the experience will attest, reading Charles Peirce's writings isn't an easy task. His prose is often dense and cryptic; sentences often begin clearly and finish vague. Some of the problem lies with the fact that until recently the primary source of Peirce's writing was *The Collected Papers of Charles Sanders Peirce*.[6] As mentioned, this eight-volume set of selections from Peirce's papers is arranged thematically and contains Peirce's writings about a single subject from different periods in his life—passages spanning many years all grouped together into close proximity. While the publication of these books was the Herculean effort of a number of dedicated Peirce scholars, the original decision to organize it thematically left something to be desired for those trying to get a sense of his overall intellectual growth from his early musings on a subject to his mature thoughts later in his life. An attempt has been made to rectify this with the advent of the Peirce Edition Project, which is an attempt to publish his writings chronologically in a projected thirty volumes called *Writings of Charles S. Peirce: A Chronological Edition*.[7] As of 2007, six volumes have been published covering Peirce's thoughts from the years 1857 through 1890, with still more than 24 years of chronological writings remaining.

Mazzagatti originally became interested in Peirce after becoming involved with Pendergraft's specification and then *The Future's Voice*, an unpublished draft in which Pendergraft wrote

> to separate out from the mire of Peirce's writings the essence of his field of argument; his premises; and as much of his argumentation as seems necessary to communicate the general character of pragmatic logic, its destined technological applications, and some practical effects that Peircian pragmatism prob-

ably must have in time toward making our individual world more intelligent than it is.[8]

Mazzagatti found it difficult to separate Pendergraft's ideas from Peirce's in the largely unquoted draft, and found that searching for quotes in the paper editions of the *Collected Papers* and the *Writings* was nearly impossible. Fortunately, she found an electronic version of *The Collected Papers of Charles Sanders Peirce*[9] and was able to electronically search to separate out Peirce quotes from Pendergraft's ideas.

However, even with this, Peirce's writings are often difficult to understand. As I've said, Peirce was a polymath, scientist, mathematician, philosopher, logician, astronomer, and it's obvious when reading him that all of these disciplines are swirling around in his head as he tries to explain some topics. Take for example this excerpted paragraph where Peirce combines ideas from math, logic, and chemistry.

> This illustration has much more pertinence to pragmatism than appears at first sight; since my researches into the logic of relatives have shown beyond all sane doubt that in one respect combinations of concepts exhibit a remarkable analogy with chemical combinations; every concept having a strict valency. (This must be taken to mean that of several forms of expression that are logically equivalent, that one or ones whose analytical accuracy is least open to question, owing to the introduction of the relation of joint identity, follows the law of valency.) Thus, the predicate "is blue" is univalent, the predicate "kills" is bivalent (for the direct and indirect objects are, grammar aside, as much subjects as is the subject nominative); the predicate "gives" is trivalent, since A gives B to C, etc.[10]

It's possible that few people have had the diverse scientific and mathematical knowledge needed to completely understand the theoretical musings of Charles Sanders Peirce, and his categorization as a philosopher was in part the result of the difficulty and uniqueness of his life's true work as a scientist. And, while his explanations often seem wildly unclear and impractical, when interpreted and implemented by Mazzagatti in a computer data structure milieu, their simplicity and elegance shine through.

So, in the remainder of this chapter and the next, I'll explain the Triadic Continuum in terms of its first practical instantiation, the rudimentary structure that Mazzagatti first visualized, which in its first application is a computer data structure designed to organize, store, and search large amounts of data. Later I'll attempt to explain how this simple and elegant structure can be used, as Peirce rightly envisioned, to explain reasoning.

Types of Data

As I explain the Triadic Continuum, I refer to data that has been collected from a particular domain, or "data universe," by which I mean the different types and formats of data that theoretically can be input into a computer. The most common data domain is "textual," which includes alphabetic characters (e.g., the letters "A" through "Z"), special characters (e.g., punctuation), and numeric data (e.g. numbers). Records of business and sales transactions are, for example, data from the universe of text.

Also, when we talk about the universe of text, including numbers, we often refer to it as "Field/Record." This refers to its format in the universe of textual data. The term "Field/Record" is a carryover from traditional database terminology, whereby a "field" represents the title of a column in a table and a record represents the structured rows within the table and contains the actual data. So, when we talk about field/record data, we're talking about data that is input from traditional tabular databases and is probably in the form of strings of text, numbers, and special characters arranged in fields within records.

However, there are other data universes and types of data that can be recorded into a Triadic Continuum, such as unstructured text, images, sound, odors, and even pressure. To understand how this works, think of pictures taken with a digital camera. For example, a digital picture of a cat may be composed of thousands of different visual dots (or pixels) arranged in a pattern within the camera's computer chip that represents the image of the cat.[11] A pixel is a single dot of light that has been assigned a value representing its color variation and a position in reference to the pixels surrounding it in order for the picture to make sense when it's viewed or printed. These values, which are just numbers, can be input into a Triadic Continuum, like textual characters, sequences, and numbers.

Another data universe is sound, which is commonly defined as a pressure or vibration transmitted through a solid, liquid, or gas through sound waves. In a computer, these waves are translated into a series of numbers (digitized) that can be manipulated mathematically, which makes it possible for a computer or CD player to play back the exact same sound time after time. An example of a universe of sound data might be quiet conversation between two people or the cacophony of sounds emanating from a stadium during an international soccer match. Because sound waves can be digitized, they can be recorded into a Triadic Continuum.

Odors are another example of a potential data universe. Odors, which we associate with our sense of smell, are simply chemical molecules that have specific characteristics, shapes, and structures. With the ability to sense and identify these individual specific characteristics and digitize them, as we can with pixels or sound waves, would enable us to construct a Triadic Continuum of odor. As strange as this may sound, a device that could record odors and recorded into a Triadic Continuum might be useful in detecting illnesses in people, such as cancer.

And finally, pressure is an entirely different data universe. By pressure I mean all of the forces that apply to a given surface. That might mean the force of my hand on a table, the weight of air on the surface of the earth, or the force of an earthquake on a tectonic plate. Since pressure is a force, it can be sensed and digitized and recorded into a Triadic Continuum.

Data Sensors

Each of the above mentioned structured and unstructured data types uses a different type of device to pick up its imprint (letters, numbers, pixels, waves, etc.) but no matter, once these electronic "patterns" are captured and digitized, they can be transmitted to the computer and a Triadic Continuum can be constructed.

In the terminology of the Triadic Continuum, these devices that are used to record the digitized data are called "sensors." We consider a sensor to be any technological device or program that detects a signal or physical condition and transforms it into a form that can be understood by a computer. A sensor could be something as simple as the keyboard on which I'm typing this sentence. As I type a letter, the electronic sensors under each key, sense the pressure and convert it to an electronic pulse that is transmitted to the computer and then on to the screen so I can see what I'm typing. A sensor might also be a photocell to pick up pixels, a thermistor to pick up changes in temperature, or even a seismometer to pick up seismic waves.

The important thing to remember is that to construct a Triadic Continuum, some type of sensor must pick up some particle of data (textual, numeric, pixel, etc.) and deliver it to a computer that contains the Triadic Continuum software.

At present, textual data is used to construct a Triadic Continuum, and in the initial invention, a sensor is nothing more than a simple computer program that takes textual and numeric data from a computer file and sends it, one character at a time to be recorded into a Triadic Continuum.

In the near future, sensors will be more sophisticated as the need to read pixels, sound, and even chemical odors becomes necessary.

The Triad—Basic Building Block of the Triadic Continuum

Now that you understand the types of data that the Triadic Continuum can use and the method used to input data, it is time to learn how the structure is constructed and what form it takes.

In general, the structure of the Triadic Continuum is defined as an interlocking forest of trees instantiated by nodes connected one to another. In computer science, tree structures are nothing new, but you'll come to see why this structure is uniquely different than all other tree structures.

The basic building block of the structure is called a "triad." A triad is composed of three components: a node and two bi-directional pointers. A single triad looks like this:

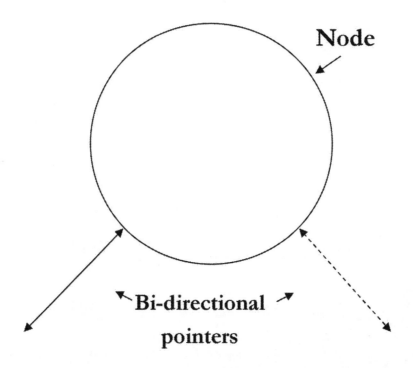

Figure 4–1

Each bi-directional pointer, called a "connexion" point to two other triads that make up a fundamental triadic unit that is composed of three nodes: a "Case node," a "Result node," and a "Sign node." The basic unit looks like the following:

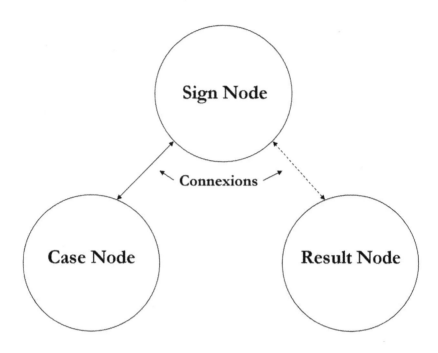

Figure 4–2

Note on the figure above that the connexion connecting the Case node to the Sign node is represented as a solid line and the other connexion connecting the Result node to the Sign node is a dotted line. Solid and dotted lines are used to make it easier to visualize the connection between a Case node and a Sign node and the connection between a Result node and the Sign node. The importance between the connexions and the solid and dotted lines will become more apparent as I explain, in later chapters, how these form the relationships between and among the nodes within the structure.

Mazzagatti believes that the structure of a triad is what Peirce envisioned when he spoke of a "spot with two tails" in his writings as he defined and explained triadic relationships.[12]

A Continuum of Triads

As triads are created and connected, a continuous structure of triads is formed, which Mazzagatti calls a "Triadic Continuum" after Peirce's use of the word "triad" and his theory of the "continuity of reasoning." When a number of triads combine, the structure takes on the form of an interlocking tree as shown in the following illustration.

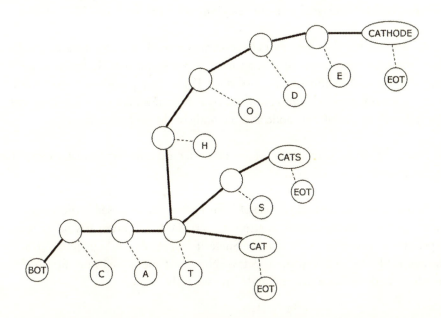

Figure 4–3

Needing a name that connotes a data structure, but not a database, Mazzagatti choose to call the Triadic Continuum, in the patents that she submitted to the Patent Office,[13] an "interlocking trees data store." In the early patents she called this data store the "K Store," or knowledge store.

Constructing a Triadic Continuum

To understand the power of the interlocking trees of the Triadic Continuum, you need to understand the process of how the structure is constructed. The process starts with the formation of a triadic unit. But, before one can be formed, something new must be experienced or sensed, such as a letter, sentence, paragraph, character, number, equation, sound, image, or other bit of data.

For the following discussion, assume that the data being sensed is the word "CAT" and that it is being experienced for the first time.

Beginning of Thought

Before a sensor sends any data, the Triadic Continuum, like the mind, is "waiting" for some new particle of data to appear. In this state of waiting, it is poised at a sensor, which Mazzagatti calls the "Beginning of Thought" or "BOT" node.

As soon as the first new particle of data is sensed, the structure is searched from the current location to determine if this specific particle has ever before been experienced in this sequence of data. If the data particle is new, in other words if it's not presently found in the structure, a new Sign node is created connecting itself to the current node and the node of the new particle.

Note that in the figures that follow, all nodes are numbered to help make the explanation easier to follow.

In our example, the first particle of information that is sensed is the letter "C." Since, as I mentioned above, this specific Triadic Continuum has never before experienced this particle, it is new. Since it's new, a new Sign node (100) is formed as shown in the diagram below. Note that the dotted lines forming the new Sign node indicate that the node isn't yet fully formed.

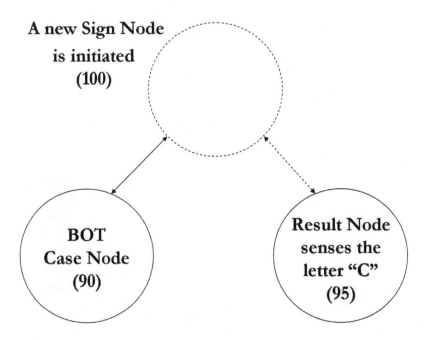

Figure 4–4

Almost simultaneously to the formation of the new Sign node, bi-directional pointers (connexions) form to connect the BOT Case node (90) and the Result node (95) to the new Sign node (100).

The Power of Connexions

One of the most powerful characteristics of the Triadic Continuum is the bi-directional connexions and how they are integral to the formation of the relationships that exist between and among the nodes of the interlocking tree and therefore represent the relationships between and among data. To see this, you need to first understand what is contained in all of the nodes of the Triadic Continuum.

All nodes contain two defining pointers and two pointer lists as shown in the following diagram.

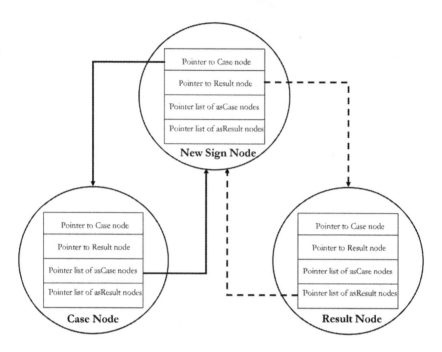

Figure 4–5

The two pointers define a new node by pointing to the sequence of nodes it represents. As shown in the diagram above, the new Sign node has a Case pointer that points back to the Case Node from which it was formed and another, the Result pointer that points back to the Result Node from which it was formed. Also within nodes are the pointer's lists of the nodes that reference it. For example, in the diagram above, the Case node contains an asCase pointer and the Result node contains an asResult pointer, both of which point to the new Sign node that was spawned by both parent nodes (Case and Result).

Refer to the following diagram as I explain how the connexions are formed using our "CAT" example.

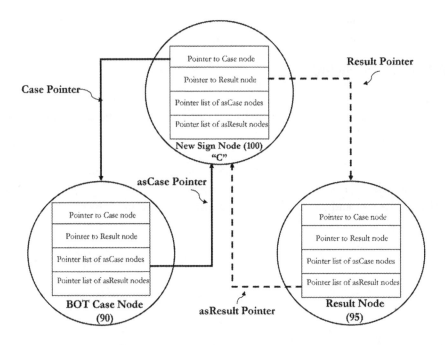

Figure 4–6

Let's begin by starting at the new Sign node (100), which is now fully formed. The new Sign node contains a pointer (called the Case pointer) that points back to the Case node (90) from which it was formed. In effect, the new Sign node (100) is identifying (and in essence "remembering") that one of its defining nodes is that specific Case node (90). As well, the Case node (90) contains a pointer list (called the asCase pointer) with a value "100" representing the identifier of the new Sign node. In effect it points to the New Sign node (100) and keeps track of the nodes which reference it as a Case node.

The new Sign node (100) also has a pointer (called the Result pointer) that points to the next node in the sequence, the Result node (95). The Result node (95) also points back to the new Sign node (100) through the asResult pointer.

The power of this is that every node created in the structure is connected to every other node in the structure through their relational links. Simply put, by using only these four simple pointers, each node in a Triadic Continua knows from whence it was formed and which nodes are formed from it—it knows its relationship within the Triadic Continuum.

Adding More Nodes

So far we've seen how a single triadic unit is formed. Now let's see what happens as other new particles of data are experienced and new triadic units are formed and connected.

The following figure shows a basic triadic unit made up of three nodes: a Case Node, Result Sign Node, and New Sign node, representing the sequence of the Case and Result, and two bi-directional pointers (the connexions).

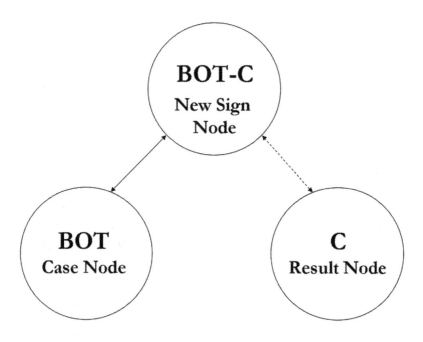

Figure 4–7

Since we're using the word "CAT" in our example and the Triadic Continuum has already experienced the letter "C," the next letter that is experienced is the letter "A." The same process occurs as before. If the letter "A" has never been experienced by this structure, a new Sign node is formed. Refer to the following figure as I explain how this happens.

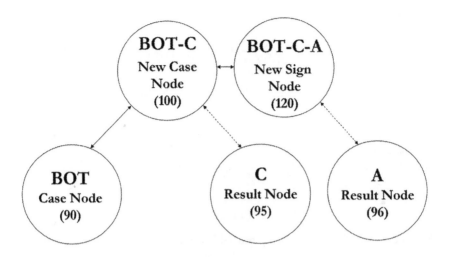

Figure 4–8

When a sensor detects the letter "A," the structure is searched to determine if the letter "A" has been experienced previously. In our example, assume that no "A" exists in the structure, so the Case node and the Result node form a new Sign node (120). Notice here that node 100 is now the Case node for a new triadic unit.

The Result node (96) and the Case node 100 send pointers to the new Sign node 120, which also sends pointers back to its Case node (100) and its Result node (96). The new Sign node (120) has a *direct* relationship with its defining nodes (100 and 96) but it has an *indirect* relationship to the other nodes (90 and 95), but only through its relation to node 100. In this way, every node is related without having to duplicate any pointers.

Now let's finish "experiencing" the word "CAT." Refer to the following figure as I explain what happens.

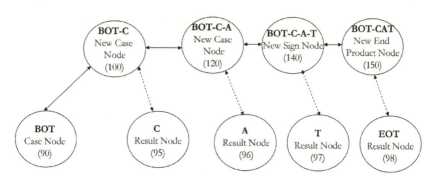

Figure 4–9

The next particle of data that is sensed is the letter "T." Again, the structure is checked to see if the letter "T" (in relation to the letters "CA") has previously been experienced. Since in our example it hasn't, a new Sign node (140) is formed with connexions to its Case node (120) and its Result node (97).

The next particle of data that is experienced is a "space." The blank space after the word "CAT" delimits the end of a word. If another sequence is sensed, a new word would start at BOT. Since, in our example, there are no others words to experience, no other triads are formed in this sequence. Two final things happen. First, an "end product node" (150) is formed that relates everything that has formed up to that point along the solid Case line. In this example, this "end product" node relates to the word "CAT." The second thing that occurs is that an "end of thought" node forms 98. It is very important to remember that there are no actual letters "C," "A," or "T" within the nodes—only pointers to their defining nodes.

Building an Interlocking Tree of Triads

Earlier in this chapter I said that the Triadic Continuum is "an interlocking forest of trees organized as nodes connected one to another." Before continuing, let's explain exactly what this means.

The Triadic Continuum actually consists of two different tree structures, one that is represented by the nodes connected by the solid lines and those connected from the dotted lines. As each node is constructed, in the manner explained above, the trees represented by the solid lines and those represented by the dotted lines are intertwined simultaneously.

The nodes connected by solid lines represent facts and those represented by dotted lines represent the relationship between and among facts. For example, in Figure 4–10 node (150) represents the "fact" that the letter "C" was experienced. Node (160) represents the fact that the word "CAT" was experienced and node (170) represents the fact of the word "CATHODE." The dotted lines represent the relationships between all of these facts.

As more data are experienced, the process continues. For example, after the word "CAT" has been experienced; assume that the next word is "CATS." Instead of constructing an entirely new tree for CATS, a branch is constructed from the previously constructed "CAT" as shown in Figure 4–10. When the word "CATHODE" is experienced, new nodes for CAT are not created because they already exist. However, since the letters "H_O_D_E" have not yet been experienced, nodes are created for them branching from the nodes for "CAT," thus forming a continuous structure of interlocking nodes. The resulting tree, as shown in Figure 4–10, is considered to be self-organizing because the structure of the forest of interlocking trees is dictated by and dependent upon the data that is received.

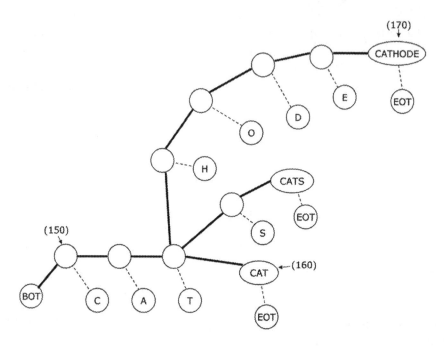

Figure 4–10

As you can see, the structure is very simple; nothing is contained in the nodes except the pointers, which form the relationships between the nodes. In other words, there is no actual data in the nodes of the structure or within computer memory. This may sound impossible, but it's key to the power of the structure. I'll talk more about this in the next chapter, but for now it's only important to understand that the triads form a continuous interlocking structure that holds the relationships between and among the facts.

Types of Nodes

As in many conceptual models, similar components having different uses are called by different names. So it is with the nodes of a Triadic Continuum. Nodes are identified differently depending on their function, position in the structure, or when in the process of construction they are identified and formed. Refer to Figure 4–11 as you read the explanation of the different types of nodes.

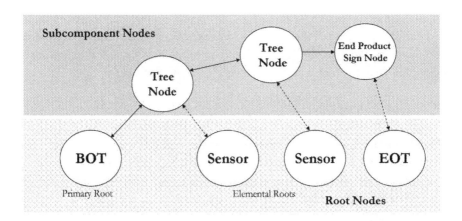

Figure 4–11

The first type of node is called an "elemental" or "root" node. Generally these are the sensors, which pick up the value of the smallest particle of data that was read. In the case of textual data, the smallest particle of data would be an alphanumeric character (A-Z and 0–9), special character (such as dollar sign, punctuation, etc.), or some other special character. These characters will vary depending on the data set being input.

Two special root nodes are the BOT (Beginning of Thought) and EOT (End of Thought) nodes. These designate the beginning and end of the data record. In our computer implementation, these act to control or delimit the sequence, allowing the program to know when a sequence begins and ends. By the way, Mazzagatti named the computer program that constructs the Triadic Continuum the "Phaneron," after Peirce's definition of "the collective total of all that is in any way or in any sense present to the mind."[14] To relate this to computers, it's all the data that is input into a Triadic Continua, or as I defined it in the previous chapter, all of the data in a data set.

Subcomponent nodes are the nodes that compose the main body of the structure. As explained earlier in this chapter, when a sensor introduces a new particle of data, a new subcomponent node is formed in association with the BOT Case node.

An end product node is a special type of subcomponent node that is the product of the last subcomponent node in a sequence and the EOT. For example, the end product node for the word "CAT," from our earlier example, is formed by the relationships between the nodes representing the beginning of thought (BOT), and the letters, "C," "A," and "T." In other words, the end product node of the CAT sequence refers to the node BOT_C_A_T_EOT.

Connecting these different types of nodes are the two different types of connexions: the Case/asCase pointers and the Result/asResult pointers. Solid lines are used to represent bidirectional connexions that point to and from subcomponent nodes along a Case or asCase path to an end product. Dotted lines are used to represent bidirectional connexions between subcomponent nodes and root nodes (sensors, EOT, or BOT) and vice versa.

As you can now see, the Triadic Continuum has at its heart a very simple composition of component parts and structural organization. However, it is exactly this elegantly simple and straightforward formation of nodes and bi-directional pointers that give it its power and flexibility. The bi-directional pointers allow association between only two nodes and within a triad; a node associates with only two other nodes. Yet because of the interlocking nature of all the nodes, a single node is indirectly associated with every node in the structure, and through this is able to form and "know" relationships within the entire structure. This conceptual model may be simple in its evolutionary organization, but complex in its ability to form and utilize relationships among all information. In the next chapter I'll explain how this unique structure was implemented in a computer data structure

5

The Triadic Continuum as Computer Structure

These are exciting conclusions. If true, they mean that Charles Peirce, late in 1886 and early 1887, invented electrical computing. Obviously it is not an invention that, as far as one knows, entered the flow of technological development at that time. It lay in cold storage until rescued ... Kenneth Ketner[1]

The previous chapter explained the simple and elegant way in which a Triadic Continuum is constructed: how new K nodes form and why the connexions are so unique and important to the structure. To illustrate the process we used a simple example, showing how the letters of the word "CAT" are learned and built into a Triadic Continuum.

While the "CAT" example is informative and illustrates the straightforward process, in this chapter I'll use more complex data to show how Triadic Continua are built with data that is input from traditional data structures, such as a list, text file, or data from tables in a relational database.

Using Computer Memory

After reading the last chapter it's easy to see that as more data is input and formed into new triads, more information about the K nodes and the connexions needs to be stored in a way that maintains the unique order and structure of the K nodes and connexions. In attempting to invent a way to do this, Mazzagatti called upon her background in computer data structures to create a structure to store all of this information about the K nodes and connexions in computer memory. Understanding a little about how a computer and computer memory works will help you understand how the Triadic Continuum is implemented in computers.

At its simplest a computer is a device that takes input data, processes it, and outputs the results to a screen, printer, or other device. Something goes in (the input) like the number "2" the special character "+" and the number "3" that you enter into your PC's calculator program, is temporarily stored (in computer memory), and something comes out (the output) after the processing, in this case the number "5."

Computer memory, or "storage," refers to the physical components of a digital computer that retain data for some period of time. Conceptually,

> a computer's memory can be viewed as a list of cells. Each cell has a numbered "address" and can store a small, fixed amount of information. This information can either be an instruction, telling the computer what to do, or data, the information which the computer is to process using the instructions that have been placed in the memory. In principle, any cell can be used to store either instructions or data.[2]

When you type the number "2" on your keyboard to enter the first number, the program controlling the calculator takes that first piece of "data" and stores it (for the moment) in a cell in the memory of the computer. The cell has an address that identifies it to the computer. When you type the plus sign "+," that piece of data is momentarily stored in a different memory cell. And when you type the number "3," that piece of data is momentarily stored in another unique memory cell. Finally, when you type the equal "=" key, the calculator program very quickly searches for the temporarily stored numbers and characters, performs the requested calculation (adding 2 plus 3), and displays the answer.

Similarly, as a triadic unit is constructed and each K node's pointers point to the defining K nodes, what happens in the computer is that each K node is assigned a cell in memory and given a unique address. The only thing retained in the computer is the address of the K node and the addresses of the referenced K nodes. This method plays to the strengths of digital computers in that a computer has the capability to retain large amounts of data in memory and is able to very quickly locate a particular bit of data in memory by using the unique memory addresses.

The basic structure of the Triadic Continuum and how it is implemented within a computer is the subject of U. S. Patents 6,961,733 and 7,158,975, written by Mazzagatti and issued in 2005 and 2007. Other patents on the technology have also been written and are pending at the U. S. Patent Office.

Bill and Tom

As Mazzagatti tried to understand and then explain the power inherent in the structure, she was struck by the thought that she needed a simple scenario to explain it. After a number of different attempts, she came up with what she called the "Bill and Tom" scenario, which I'll use in this chapter as I explain how the Triadic Continuum is used as a computer data structure.

The "Bill and Tom" scenario is an example of how the Triadic Continuum works in the Field/Record universe. As you'll remember, a Field/Record universe contains alphanumeric data and control characters that may be input from a traditional database and consists of letters, words, numbers, and special characters arranged in fields within records. This data is also known as "structured" because it is input from traditional databases in the form of tables of data structured in rows and columns.

The scenario contains only nine records from the Field/Record universe. The following table shows the data for these nine records, which are from a fictitious furniture company and refer to the number of items sold by individual salespersons in different regions of the country. These data records are input into a computer system one character at a time in a continuous stream of data.

Salesperson	Day	Product	Transaction	State
Bill	Tuesday	Sofa	Sold	PA
Bill	Tuesday	Sofa	Sold	PA
Bill	Tuesday	Sofa	Sold	PA
Bill	Monday	Table	Sold	NJ
Bill	Monday	Sofa	Trial	PA
Tom	Monday	Sofa	Sold	PA
Tom	Monday	Sofa	Sold	PA
Tom	Monday	Table	Trial	NJ
Bill	Tuesday	Sofa	Sold	PA

Figure 5–1

The first record that is input is "_Bill_Tuesday_Sofa_Sold_PA_" (the underscore before, between and after the words represents a blank space or a control character used to delimit the beginning and end of a field variable and record.) Before beginning to explain how the structure is formed for these records, let me say that you must assume that the sensors for the individual letters and control characters that make up these field records already exist in the structure. In other words, there is any number of control characters and 26 possible elements (the 26 individual letters of the English alphabet) of the particle universe that have already been experienced. So there's no need to show these letters being formed. So the process starts with the sequence of letters as words are being experienced.

The first value learned is the word "Bill," since the first record begins with the field value "Bill."

As you'll remember from the last chapter, as soon as something is experienced and is perceived as "new" (or never having been experienced before,) a new Sign K node "BOT-Bill" is created. This first new K node is named "BOT-Bill" and not just "Bill" because it is the beginning of a thought that will eventually represent our first record "_Bill_Tuesday_Sofa_Sold_PA_." You may find it helpful to refer to the next figure as you read the next few paragraphs.

Next, the sensor set experiences the word "Tuesday" for the first time in association with the word "Bill," so a new Sign K node is formed and represents "BOT-Bill-Tuesday." Just to refresh your memory, the Case K node for "BOT-Bill-Tuesday" is the K node that represents the "BOT-Bill" K node and the Result K node for it is that K node that represents the just experienced "Tuesday." This process continues until all of the fields in the first record are experienced.

When the last word (data sequence of particles) in this record is experienced, an end of record control character is experienced. This control character, which may be any character not a part of the alphanumeric character set, is there to delimit the end of record. When this occurs two things happen: an end of thought (EOT) node forms, which then, with the last asCase K node formed (the BOT-Bill-Tuesday-Sofa-Sold-PA node) forms the end of thought node, which in this example is, "BOT-Bill-Tuesday-Sofa-Sold-PA-EOT. The following diagram shows the structure for the first record.

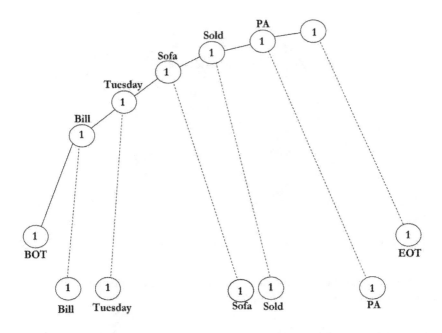

Figure 5–2

Counters

Notice that included within each K node is a number; in the example above each K node contains the number "1." In the computer program that constructs the K structure, this number represents the count of how many times this value (letter, special character, word, number, value or sequence) has been experienced. So, besides the four pointers found in each K node, that we've already explained, each K node also contains a "counter" to record the number of times each K node has been experienced, as shown below.

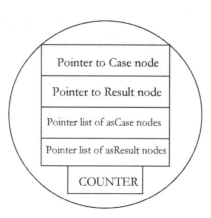

Figure 5–3

As you'll see in the next chapter, these counters are important in the current implementation of the Triadic Continuum in computers.

Now let's see what happens when the second record is experienced. The second record contains the exact field values as the first record: "_Bill_Tuesday_Sofa_Sold_PA_." The following diagram shows the structure after this record is added.

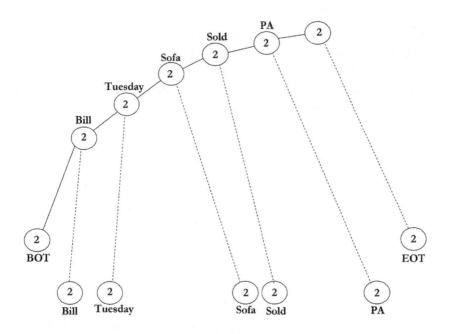

Figure 5–4

Since the record was already experienced, no new Sign K nodes need be formed. The only thing that happens is that the counters are incremented by "1". As more records are experienced the counters for each K node increments in the same order as the K nodes are formed. By that I mean that in this figure, the BOT was incremented to the number "2," then the "Bill" Result K node was incremented to "2," then the BOT-Bill sign node was incremented to "2" and so forth until the last "end product" node was incremented to "2" after EOT.

Since the third record again contains the same field values as the first two records, no new K nodes are formed; again, the counters are incremented, this time to "3."

The fourth record, "_Bill_Monday_Table_Sold_NJ_" is new and has not been previously experienced. In this record "Bill" is the same as the last three records, but the second value "Monday" has never been experienced in association with Bill before, so a new Sign K node is formed to represent the sequence "BOT-Bill-Monday," new path where "BOT-Bill" is the Case K node. The other new sign K nodes are formed beginning with "Table," which has not been experienced before, all the way to "NJ" and on to the end product nodes and EOT. Notice in the next figure that since this is the fourth record with the value "Bill," the "BOT-Bill" node's counter is incremented to "4" while the "BOT-Bill-Monday" node is only incremented to "1" since this is the first time Bill-Monday has been experienced. As well, note that the counters for "BOT-Bill-Tuesday" remains at "3" since this fourth record does not included the value "Tuesday."

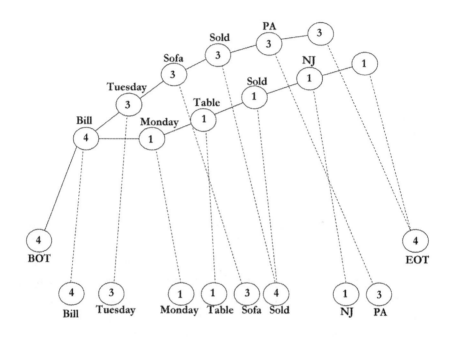

Figure 5–5

The fifth record is slightly different with "_Bill_Monday_Sofa_Trial_PA_." Since Bill has been experienced, "BOT-Bill" is incremented to "5." Because "Monday" has been experienced once before, it is incremented to "2." From there, the values are new to the sequence Bill-Monday, so a new sign K node path is formed as shown in the next figure.

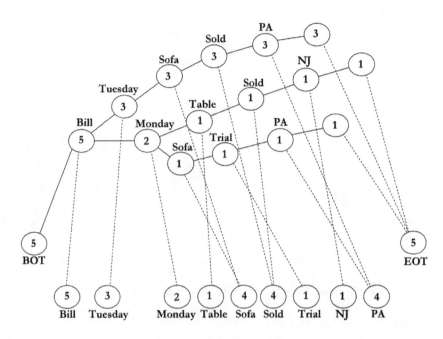

Figure 5–6

Record six is "_Tom_Monday_Sofa_Sold_PA_." Since "Tom" has never been experienced, a new path of sign K nodes are formed, as shown below.

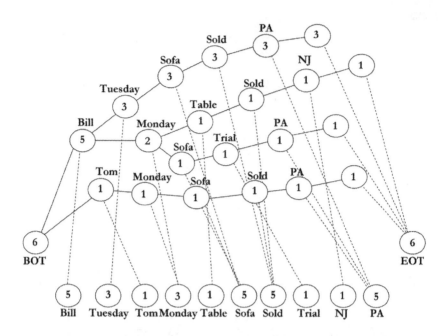

Figure 5–7

Record seven is "_Tom_Monday_Sofa_Sold_PA_." Since it's the same as record six, only the K node counters in that path are incremented to "2."

Record eight is "_Tom_Monday_Table_Trial_NJ_." Since Tom and Monday have already been experienced, their counters are incremented, but because "Table" has never been experienced with Tom-Monday, a new sign K node path is formed, as shown in the next figure.

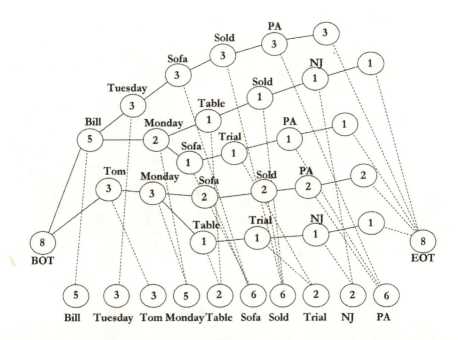

Figure 5–8

The ninth (and last) record is "_Bill_Tuesday_Sofa_Sold_PA_." This record is the same as the first three records and since it's already been experienced, only the counters of the K nodes in the path are incremented as shown in the following figure; no new records need to be formed.

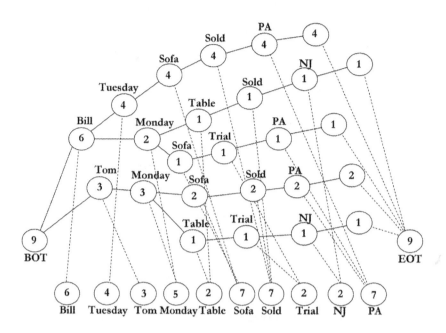

Figure 5–9

As you can see, the counters in only the Bill_Tuesday_Sofa_Sold_PA record have been increased. So to this point, the illustration above reflects the resulting Triadic Continuum for the nine-record data set that we began with. We could go on adding records, but the process is the same: sensor experiencing new data, the structure being traversed to see if the data is unique, if unique new K nodes are added, and if already a part of the structure, the counter will be increased.

No Data and No Duplication

Before continuing, it's important to reiterate two things mentioned earlier. First, the fact that K nodes in the Triadic Continuum contain nothing but pointers and counters, no actual data exists in the structure or within computer memory. For example, the words "Bill," "Tuesday," "Sofa," "Sold," or "PA," can't be found in the actual structure or in computer memory, only the pointers to the K nodes representing them, and possibly a number in a counter. The only place the actual data exists is in the original records that are read into the Triadic Continuum. Once the K nodes and connexions are formed, the only thing that exists is the relationships between the K nodes, which in effect represent the relationship between the particular bits of data. Knowing that "Tuesday" comes after "Bill" in the structure allows one to know that there is an inherent relationship between Bill and Tuesday. We'll talk about the importance of these relationships later.

The second important thing is that there is no duplication within the structure. All of the individual letters that make up the words are represented only once in a Triadic Continuum. Similarly, all of the words are only represented once. And if sentences are input into a Triadic Continuum, they too only exist once. Once a structure has been built for a letter, a word, a sentence, etc., it isn't duplicated.

Having said that nothing is duplicated, you might have noticed that some bits of data seem to be duplicated in the Bill and Tom scenario. For example, in Figure 5–10 there are duplicate portions: K nodes "Sold" and "PA," shown highlighted in black.

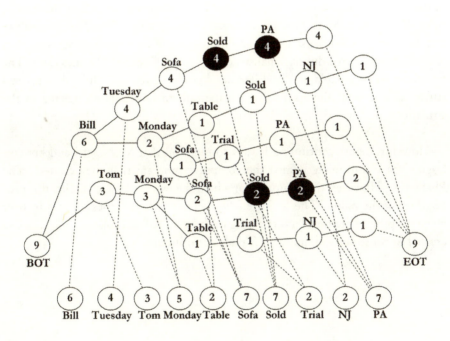

Figure 5–10

This contradiction is explained by saying that the Phaneron software that exists as I write this book is a rudimentary version of what it will eventually become. By this I mean that Mazzagatti has initially implemented a simpler version of the eventual software that will, in theory, recognize duplicated data and create a structure that does not duplicate K nodes. Mazzagatti and her colleagues have already identified, on paper, a mechanism to accomplish this; it's only a matter of time before it is implemented. However, the present structure of the Phaneron is still extremely powerful and elegantly simple, so the remainder of this book will explain the structure as it currently exists and is implemented today.

Dimensional Data Structures

The more Mazzagatti diagrammed different Triadic Continua and thought more about the implications of its structure and how the K nodes are organized, the more she saw that the structure is different from simple two-dimensional data structures; it's really three-dimensional. And, as she came to realize, it is this dimensionality that makes the Triadic Continuum much more powerful and easy to use than two-dimensional data structures and other structures that claim to be three-dimensional. So to fully understand the power of the Triadic Continuum, one must understand the strengths and limitations of two-dimensional structures and what a true three-dimensional structure can provide that 2D ones can't. The following chapter explains the difference between two- and three-dimensional structures and why dimensionality is important to how data are related in the structure.

However, before continuing I want to mention that Mazzagatti and her colleagues' have informally named the computer program that they created "The Phaneron." However, the company for which she works plans to market this program using the name "The K Store." So, if I use either of these names in later chapters, please note that I am referring to the same software application that was created to construct and query the Triadic Continuum.

6

Realizing Knowledge in the Triadic Continuum

Where is the wisdom we have lost in knowledge?/Where is the knowledge we have lost in information? T.S. Eliot[1]

It is perfectly true that we can never attain a knowledge of things as they are. We can only know their human aspect. But that is all the universe is for us. Charles Peirce[2]

In this chapter I'll explain how knowledge is realized from within the structure of a Triadic Continuum. I'm purposely not using words like "found," "located," or "discovered" to refer to how knowledge is detected or made known; the words *realizing* and *knowledge* are used in a very precise way. Since knowledge is the easier of the two, I'll begin with that and explain what I mean by *realizing* a little later in the chapter.

What Is Knowledge?

Since the beginning of recorded history, mankind has been intrigued by the idea of knowledge. Whether it was the early Egyptians, Chinese, or Greeks, each culture explored what is meant by knowledge and talked about how knowledge is gained. More than 2,000 years ago, Aristotle dealt with the uncertainty of knowledge by attempting to categorize knowledge based on empirical observations.[3] This quest to understand the meaning and scope of human knowledge, as well as how the mind acquires, builds, and retains knowledge continues unabated today. In fact, advances in the fields of cognitive science, the study of the mind or intelligence, and neurobiology, the study of the structure, function and behavior of the nervous system are commonly reported on in the general media. But, what do we mean by knowledge and what is its connection to the structure we call the Triadic Continuum?

Systems theorist Dr. Russell Ackoff has defined the content of the human mind as a continuum that ranges from data, information, knowledge, understanding, to wisdom, and posits that the first four deal with things that have been or are known and that wisdom deals with things in the future.[4] Being aware of how he defines these terms will help you understand more clearly what can be truly known from the data that is in the structure of a Triadic Continuum.

Data is defined as being raw; something that just exists and which has no significance beyond its existence, for example, a word, number, or image is a datum. Of itself, the number 5551212 is just pure data—it has no significance, no meaning. Think of information as data that is processed and is useful; it provides the answers to "who," what," "where," and "when" questions. It is data whose meaning derives from its relationship to other data. Its meaning can be useful or not. Knowing that the number 5551212 may have a dash between the 5 and the 1, or 555–1212, brings meaning to the datum 5551212. Adding a dash after the third number brings the entire string of data into relation with other data that share the same format, and in doing so, brings meaning to this specific formatted string and answers the "what" question with the answer "a telephone number."

Knowledge can be thought of as an application of data and information to answer the "how" questions. The intent of knowledge is to be useful; it has a purpose or use. Knowing that one can access emergency services by calling 911 provides a purpose for the information; it provides us with knowledge. Simply put, knowledge is bringing data or chunks of information into relationship with one another.

Understanding is a higher-level process that makes new knowledge from previous knowledge. When one understands the relationships between data, information, and knowledge, one can begin answering the "why" questions.

And finally, *wisdom* makes the best available use of knowledge and understanding, as well as other moral and ethical mores and experiences to give one understanding where there was no understanding before—it helps one to ask questions "to which there is no (easily achievable) answer, and in some cases, to which there can be no humanly-known answer."[5]

Finding Information in Databases

In life, true greatness comes from the true understanding of our knowledge and the attainment of wisdom comes from true understanding, but in terms of today's data structures, the quest to obtain realistic and accurate knowledge should not be minimized. Being able to find what one is looking for in a traditional database is the fundamental raison d'être of the structure and the methods used to search and query it. However, finding data and information isn't the only thing of importance; think of the benefit of discovering the knowledge hidden in a data structure. Today, most of the knowledge that a company or organization has is held in the heads of its employees; they may have entered some of this knowledge—but not all—into word processing documents, spreadsheets, and databases, and what has been entered may be difficult to get to. Plus, the amount of data being stored in databases today is staggering.

Companies who use databases in their business—and it's safe to say that this includes the Fortune 1000 companies, universities and scientific labs, large charitable organizations, banking and financial institutions, and even eBay—currently store the vast majority of their transactional, customer, experimental, and employee data in relational databases. However, besides storing and retrieving data for everyday business use, most of these companies have entire departments dedicated to understanding what exactly is in all the multi-gigabyte amounts of data they have stored in their databases. Also, and probably most importantly, the larger, more successful companies attempt to make business predictions and formulate strategy based on, in part, the best information available to them in their own databases.

Because of the tremendous stakes involved in today's chaotic business environment, the company with the best understanding of its day-to-day operations, its customers wants and needs, and how it spends its own money, will likely prosper in today's global competition. And, what's true of businesses is also true of charitable, scientific, and other organizations—those who intimately understand their own operation, the needs of those they serve, and can find the information they need are in the best possible position for success.

Companies and organizations that understand that making informed decisions is based on an intimate detailed knowledge of their business practices employ experts to help them analyze and understand the information found in their databases. Often they employ experts in "data modeling" and "data mining" to help them uncover and discover the strengths and weaknesses of their practices and look for hidden and emerging trends in their data.

The practitioners of data modeling work to define techniques "that records the inventory, shape, size, contents, and rules of data." Their ultimate goal is to capture a "representation of something that exists" within the data.[6] This "something" cannot be effectively represented without knowing how data are related to one another—not just the easily observed relationships, but also the more subtle or obtuse relationships.

Also interested in the relationships within data are those who practice data mining. Data mining, also referred to as "knowledge discovery," is a branch of database computing in which data is analyzed in different ways to categorize and summarize the relationships that exist within the data and information. In trying to extract hidden knowledge, data-mining activities attempt to identify the patterns or correlations that exist within large volumes of data.

It's All About the Structure

At the core of data mining and data modeling is the fact that they are both interested in uncovering the knowledge within data and information. However, it's increasingly clear that both of these disciplines are having a difficult time doing this.

In traditional data structures, data is entered in a fixed format (tables, lists, or trees) so that the data can be easily, reliably, and consistently found. And, in a very real sense, data and information are discovered; programmers must write programs to enable users to query the data and write other specialized programs to search the distinct data structure in a prescribed way, searching for bits of data and particles of information until eventually something which matches the query criteria is found.

However, and this is significant, in the Triadic Continuum, data are learned into a structure whose format and organization systematically build a record or recording of the associations and relations between the particles of data. Besides that, the physical structure of the Triadic Continuum shapes the methods to obtain information and knowledge from the structure. So, instead of data and information being "found," "analyzed," or "discovered," it is already there waiting to be "realized." About this incredibly unique aspect of the Triadic Contin-uum, we often say that "it's all in the structure." By this we mean that the format and organization of the Triadic Continuum not only hold the representation of the data, but also the associations and relations between the data and the methods to obtain information and knowledge.

And while traditional databases deal mostly with finding data and informa-tion, the focus of the Triadic Continuum is in knowledge, acquisition of useful and purposeful knowledge. And with that, comes the potential to create true understanding and real wisdom.

The remainder of this chapter explains how the organization and the dimen-sionality of the K structure allows for the "realizing" of the knowledge that is inherently within the data recorded in it.

Dimensionality

The term "dimensionality" is used here to denote the difference between a two-dimensional data structure and one that exists in three dimensions. You probably saw the Bill and Tom diagrams in the last chapter as being two-dimensional, with the structure drawn from left to right (length) and bottom to top (height); seem-ingly with no depth. However, the structure of the Triadic Continuum is actually three-dimensional. And as you'll see, its three-dimensionality brings a whole dif-ferent aspect to the structure, how it's used, and how knowledge is realized within it.

Two Dimensional Structures

As explained in Chapter 3, traditional "relational databases use a structure of rows and columns to store data, in tables of records."[7] However, "tables are just one type of data structure that can be used to organize data; others include data files, lists, strings, arrays, records, as well as tree structures."[8] One thing that all of these structures have in common is that they are two-dimensional and while ubiquitous in the world of data structures, and not without advocates, two-dimensional structures are known to be difficult to maintain and highly ineffi-cient.

Technology and database analysts write that the inherent nature of two-dimensional structures is a primary cause of its difficulty to maintain.

The problem with relational databases is that the fundamental data structure they use is a two-dimensional table. In relational theory, data is supposed to be organized into normalized tables—that is, the data is supposed to be organized in such a way that there is only one way to get to it, allowing the developer to eliminate redundancy and ensure that changes to the data are consistent. This design technique was introduced to ensure that relational tables contained independent sets of data that were related only by a key.[9]

The problem with this technique is that it is not capable of representing all the relationships and structures that data can have. Also, storing data in this way causes the programmer to break apart the data record before storing it in the database and then recombine it in order to use it.

It is as if, in storing a car in the garage, you take the doors off, remove the seats, take off the wheels and so on. It is time-consuming and it makes no sense.[10]

Finding information in a two-dimensional structure, such as a table, may also be difficult because while a "table has a fixed column order, rows themselves are inherently unordered."[11] This leads to difficulty in representing, storing, and accessing some fairly common types of data in two-dimensional structures, such as tables and trees. For example, a bus route is simply an ordered list of bus stops. However, ordered data, such as the stops in a bus route need to be further indexed in order to make it easier to locate in an unordered list of a table.

Another common example is a bill of materials–a product and its components in a manufacturing system. The components themselves may have components that in turn may have components and so on. A relational database table of all parts will not express the relationships of the parts to the parts of parts, and so on. These relationships express important data. To query a database for a product and all its components should be straightforward. A relational database structure makes the developer's job of answering this simple query, unnecessarily complex and difficult.[12]

Common two-dimensional trees also introduce complex problems for programmers building procedures for storing and searching these structures. Tomes have been written by mathematicians and computer analysts on the computational procedures used to traverse and locate a bit of specific data within a tree. For example, the textbook, *Introduction to Algorithms*[13] contains over 1000 pages of strategies and procedures for sorting, ordering, and searching two-dimensional data structures. While practitioners of the discipline will tell you that it's all part of the job, it's not an easy job.

Creating Workarounds

In Chapter 3 we also talked about how database cubes were originally designed to analyze large groups of ordered records in ways that would allow a user to see the data organized and presented in a specific fashion. We mentioned that cubes arrange data from relational databases in arrays that allow the user to view the data from different perspectives or dimensions. Data cubes can be thought of as a way to view in three dimensions two-dimensional data. In fact

> Data cubes are multidimensional extensions of 2-D tables, just as in geometry a cube is a three-dimensional extension of a square. The word *cube* brings to mind a 3-D object, and we can think of a 3-D data cube as being a set of similarly structured 2-D tables stacked on top of one another.
>
> But data cubes aren't restricted to just three dimensions. Most online analytical processing (OLAP) systems can build data cubes with many more dimensions—Microsoft SQL Server 2000 Analysis Services, for example, allows up to 64 dimensions. We can think of a 4-D data cube as consisting of a series of 3-D cubes, though visualizing such higher-dimensional entities in spatial or geometric terms can be a problem.[14]

And while more powerful than a relational database, the extended timeframes to construct and modify cubes, their increased storage requirements, and other thorny technical issues, don't always make them the most effective solution. In effect, cubes are workarounds, or a temporary fix for the weaknesses of traditional databases.

A Three Dimensional Structure

The remainder of this chapter deals with the 3D nature of the Triadic Continuum and what it is about this multidimensionality that makes it exponentially more "powerful" than structures that by their organization can only store, hold, and search data in two dimensions.

Drawing the Structure

As Mazzagatti began to realize the potential power of her discovery, she found that she had some difficulty drawing the structure that was before her mind. Because of her background in computers, some memorable life experiences, interests, and her education in cognitive learning theory, she visualized the structure as a combination of an electronic circuit board and a network of brain cells. If you've ever watched a science program on television where the brain is discussed, you've undoubtedly seen images of neurons lighting up along their paths as the subject thinks, talks, sings, or imagines. This image, coupled with images of computer circuit boards was what Mazzagatti saw in her mind as she put pencil to paper.

Mazzagatti was also quite familiar with tree structures that are comprised of nodes, and even with trees that used bi-directional pointers. So, she attempted to draw the structure she saw in her mind as a hybrid of neurons, trees, and electronic circuits. What appeared on paper was a tree structure with interlocking nodes.

Almost immediately she ran into a problem. When trying to interpret the structure on paper, she found she needed a way to differentiate between the lines that represented the Case and asCase pointers (the recording of the sequence) and those representing the Result and asResult pointers (the relationship links). One of her original drawings looked like the following, which is a structure representing the words "quick," "quiet," and "quack."

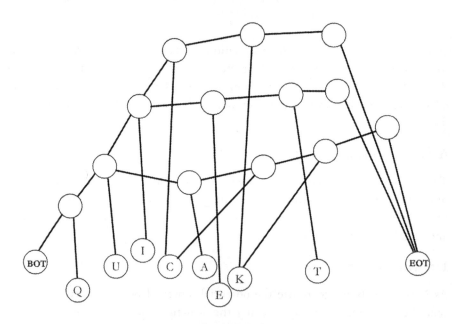

Figure 6–1

With all solid lines, Mazzagatti quickly got confused as she added more nodes and the picture got more and more complex. Her frustration came in trying to visualize how to traverse the structure to realize the answers to questions about information in the structure. She intuitively understood that the difference between the pointers was of major importance, but was at a loss to figure out how to best represent the difference. Eventually she tried drawing one line a different color and while that worked, it was impractical as she sat and drew structures on the ubiquitous yellow legal pads she uses to record the different ideas and inventions that stem from this structure. She finally hit upon a very simple solution: use solid and dotted lines to represent the two different types of bi-directional connexions. She decided to draw all of the lines that represented the Case/asCase pointers as solid lines and use dotted lines to represent the pointers for the Result/asResult connexions as shown in the following "quick, quiet, quack" diagram.

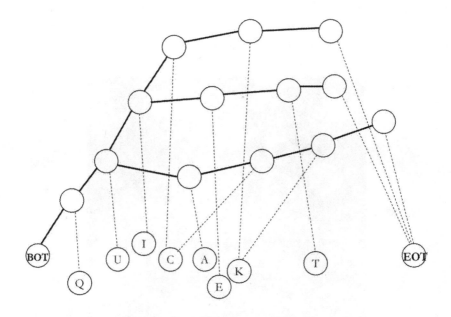

Figure 6–2

This simple serendipitous solution laid the groundwork for her being able to explain the structure in terms of its three-dimensionality. These dotted lines help to clearly visualize the difference between the two-dimensionality of traditional databases and the three-dimensionality of the Triadic Continuum.

Visualizing Three-Dimensional Structures

Looking at any diagram of the Triadic Continuum from the "Bill and Tom" scenario and you might not see at first that the structure is three-dimensional. For one thing, it's drawn flat on the page and so in effect it is shown in only two dimensions. If you're someone who can normally look at geometric shapes in a textbook or on a piece of paper and instinctively visualize it in three dimensions, seeing not only its length and height, but also sensing its depth, you'll have little problem seeing how the Triadic Continuum is three-dimensional. However, if you see it only as a flat drawing without depth, it may take other visual clues to help you see it as three-dimensional.

The following illustration is a representation of a simple Triadic Continuum shown as three-dimensional. Notice that the bottom leftmost node is the "Beginning of Thought" (BOT) node. The other nodes along the Case/asCase solid line stretch out into the space away from the BOT node and the sensors appear to be to the lower right of the BOT node attached to nodes with dotted lines.

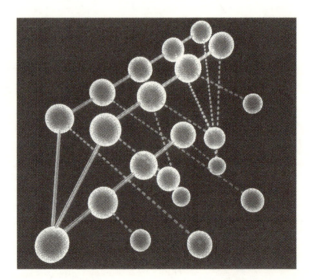

Figure 6–3

Since I'm not sitting next to you as you read this, you may be asking yourself what's the big deal with dotted lines and 3D. Good question! Here's the simple answer. The dotted lines enable you to see the three-dimensionality of the structure and that's what makes it so easy to identify the types of relationships and connections between and among data sequences that naturally occur in the structure of a Triadic Continuum. Simply said, relationships are the big deal; they are unquestionably the most important concept to understand the power of the Triadic Continuum and its ability to uncover specific and non-specific associations within knowledge.

That being said, the discussion of the relationships that naturally occur within the Triadic Continuum covers nearly all of the remainder of this book. However, before getting to that discussion, I'd like to first talk about three other important concepts.

Constraint, Context, and Focus

As with any new theory or field of scientific endeavor, the discoverer and early promoters find the need to coin or redefine terms to explain the discovery; the same can be said for Mazzagatti's Triadic Continuum. However, it wasn't simply a matter of defining new terms where none before existed. We've also had to assess Peirce's use of certain terms and either attempt to explain his terminology in modern terms and in other cases actually prove that what he was saying was illustrating a concept better illustrated using the Triadic Continuum. We have found that with an understanding of the concepts surrounding the Triadic Continuum that much of Peirce's writings become clearer—it's as though he were attempting to define a new field of study, where he was the sole practitioner, and was a hundred years ahead of his time.

In defining her terminology, Mazzagatti has attempted to use Peirce's terms wherever possible. However, in some cases she either had to invent new terminology or, in the case of computers, adapt existing database or computer term. And finally, in some cases she redefined existing terms with slightly new and different meaning.

There are three terms that she often uses when discussing the Triadic Continuum: "constraints," "context," and "focus." Each has its own common meaning as well as a meaning that makes sense in terms of computers and databases.

Constraints

The simplest definition of the term "constraint" is the act of limiting. In our discussion of the Triadic Continuum, we often talk about constraining the data set to only those values we're interested in. As you may remember from the discussion in Chapter 3, a "data set" is a collection of related records. In that previous chapter we used IRS taxpayer data as an example of a large real-world data set.

In its current software implementation, the data that is loaded into the Triadic Continuum most often comes from traditional databases as a large data set—for example, a data set that contains all taxpayer information for a given year. The records in this data set are structured in two-dimensional tables composed of rows and columns, with each cell in the table being called a field. Finally, each field contains a value. For example, "0" is one possible value for the field "Exemptions."

In the taxpayer data set there are hundreds of fields with thousands of potential values. And, each record may contain fields that are potentially duplicated millions of times throughout the database—one (or more) records for each individual taxpayer. It's not hard to envision the complexity of this type of tabular database.

Whereas in traditional databases, the value for each field in each record is loaded and stored, in the structure of the Triadic Continuum, only the relationships between the nodes and the number in the counters are stored. But, even in the elegantly simple structure of the Triadic Continuum, "lots of data" is still "lots of data." And one drawback of huge amounts of data is slow performance when searching the structure, be it traditional databases or the Triadic Continuum. This of course presents a problem to those who need to query and search databases. It has long been known that traditional business, governmental, and scientific databases contain multi-gigabytes of data and are not only plagued with the problem of slow query performance, but also with the additional effort and time needed to modify the structure of the traditional database to make it more efficient to query.

In defense, database analysts and programmers have designed methods to narrow a data set in order to constrain the data to a smaller sub-set that enables faster searching. For example, if one were looking for all taxpayers in Nebraska with the last name "Anderson," it would be easier to first constrain the data set to limit the search to those records that contain Nebraska, then to search for the name Anderson.

If you have ever used a spreadsheet program, like Microsoft Excel, you may be familiar with a concept similar to constraining data, or "filtering." For those who have never used Excel it is an electronic spreadsheet, which is composed of a grid or table of columns and rows. Once data are entered into the grid it can be manipulated, such as alphabetically sorting text data or numerically sorting numbers. Numbers can also be calculated. People use electronic spreadsheets for everything from managing their monthly bills to managing customer and financial data for good-sized businesses. Spreadsheet programs like Excel use filtering to allow users to hide data within the spreadsheet. Only data that match your criteria is displayed and that which doesn't match is hidden from view; hidden data isn't deleted or lost, just hidden from sight. This is particularly handy when the amount of data is too great to be easily manageable, and by manageable, I mean easily seen. Filtering is also used when the amount of data is so great that working with all of it at once takes a lot of time. For example, assume that you run a small business selling some product over the Internet and you keep all of your customer and transaction data in a spreadsheet, similar to the top screen in the following figure.

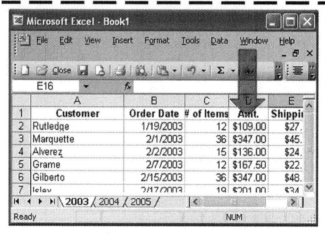

Figure 6–4

Assume also that you want to offer a special promotion to your best customers, say, those who have purchased over $100, out of your total customer base of 350 people. Keeping records for 350 customers is just small enough to manage in a spreadsheet, but a little too large to view all at one time. Using a filter, you can hide the data for the customers who have purchased less than $100 worth of merchandise and see only those who have purchased more than $100. The data for those purchasing less than $100 isn't lost, merely hidden from view. The lower screen in Figure 6–4 shows what the same spreadsheet might look like after filtering only those purchases over $100.

By constraining data in the Triadic Continuum, you are doing something like filtering in spreadsheets, you're limiting the data you want to look at and work with to a smaller group of records (paths).

Before explaining the power of constraining data in a Triadic Continuum, let's briefly compare how quick it is to search a Triadic Continuum for a specific piece of data versus a traditional relational database. In traditional database structures and cubes, fast search speed is achieved by caching the data values in memory. Then, each time a search needs to be performed, the computer has only to go to the cached memory and search there for pre-defined values and results. It may seem quick, but you're sacrificing relevancy for speed. However, with the Triadic Continuum there's no need to cache results; each calculation performed on data can be performed in real-time on data that is constantly and dynamically being fed into the structure. Instead of caching values and performing canned queries, one can perform "cold queries" on the data in a Triadic Continuum. As explained in Chapter 5, because of its unique inherent indexing, the Triadic Continuum can search the data on the fly and find the answer immediately. The programmers who worked on the original version of the Triadic Continuum software have found that cold queries with a Triadic Continuum are as fast or faster than cached queries in traditional data structures.

Therefore, besides saying that the amount of data is a factor in the speed at which data are searched, even without constraining data, the Triadic Continuum is faster than a traditional relational database. When you then limit or constrain the data, it dramatically increases the speed and efficiency of a search.

In the world of the Triadic Continuum, "constraint" is considered a variable value (a value that you have the ability to change, e.g., from number of tax exemptions to the state of residence) that limits a data set to only those records containing it. When constraining the data in a Triadic Continuum, you're not limited to only one field; one or more values can be selected to limit the fields that you want isolated for analysis.

So, how is this accomplished in the structure of the Triadic Continuum? It's a lot simpler than you might expect. In a traditional database, someone must create a data cube to constrain data. As explained in Chapter 3, queries are limited to the exact data in the cube at the time it is created. Therefore, every time the data in the cube changes, the cube must be recreated. Therefore a cube must be specifically designed to a specific type of constraint and if a different type of constraint is needed, the cube must be must be modified or redesigned. Using the Bill and Tom furniture store data for example, one may want to see only those transactions that occurred in a specific state for a specific product. They would have to constrain the data set to only those records that contained data about transactions that occurred in Pennsylvania and were for sales of sofas. Using traditional technology, a programmer would modify or redesign the cube to limit the data to only those records that contain Pennsylvania. Then a query could be defined that searched those records for the item, "sofa." If it were decided that, instead, the state of interest was "New Jersey," the cube would have to be redesigned again. It's easy to see that this takes time and costs money to keep redesigning data cubes. Plus, creating a comprehensive set of cubes to cover all possible combinations of variables would result in an unwieldy, large cube. And still, the inherent two-dimensional nature of traditional database structures complicates and slows down the way the table is searched. As mentioned earlier, because of difficulties such as just described, database analysts have had to invent methods and a structure like data warehouses and data cubes to "workaround" the inherent flaws of the relational database. But, as these analysts and their chief information officers will attest, data cubes, indexes, and other methods are expensive and take more time than most businesses want to invest.

Given the structure of the Triadic Continuum, there is no need to create, modify or redesign indexes, schema, or multi-dimensional data cubes. Refer to the following diagram as I explain what happens.

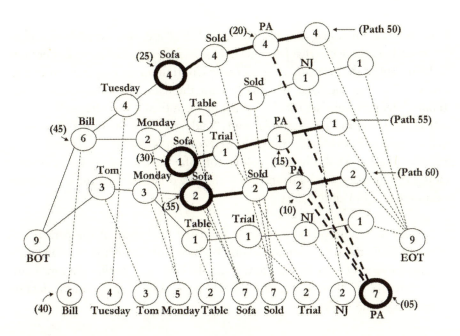

Figure 6–5

In the structure of the Triadic Continuum, we only need to locate the root node for Pennsylvania "PA" (05) and trace the Result/asResult paths (dotted lines) to the "PA" sub-component nodes it connects to, in this case (nodes 10, 15, and 20). We then trace the Case/asCase path (solid lines) from each of these nodes in both directions until a node representing "Sofa" is located. Now, all that we need to do to find the number of sofas sold in Pennsylvania is to record the number found in the counter, and when all are found, add them together. In our example, tracing the dotted line from the "PA" root node found three paths (paths 50, 55, and 60). Then tracing the solid line for those three paths we found three occurrences (nodes) representing "sofa" (nodes 25, 30, and 35) When we add up the numbers in the counters of these sofa nodes, we get a count of seven.

We might assume that seven sofas were sold in Pennsylvania. However, if you carefully look at the paths, you'll notice that between the nodes that represent "PA" and the nodes that represent "Sofa" there's a node in two paths representing "Sold," but also one occurrence of a node representing "Trial." Therefore, we really didn't determine the number of sofas that were sold in Pennsylvania.

If you had attempted this in a traditional database, you would have had to construct something external from the database, such as a data cube. But because of the nature of the structure of the Triadic Continuum we only have to change how we constrain the data. We simply limit the data using two different constraints: "Pennsylvania" and "Sold." What happens then is that after we locate the root nodes for both "Pennsylvania" and "Sold," we trace the dotted lines from each of them and only look at the paths that contain both of them. Then we trace the solid lines, as we did before, looking for sofa. In this case we find that after adding the numbers in the counters for these two nodes, the sum is six, or six sofas were sold in Pennsylvania.

By only searching paths that derive from the root node of the constrained value, we limit the data without having to change the structure or create additional external structures. In our above example, if we want to find out how many items were sold in New Jersey, all we would have to do is constrain the data on "New Jersey" and "Sold."

Constraints show one of the tremendous strengths of the Triadic Continuum: because the structure contains a recording of all of the relationships, it is what it is and does not have to be modified to find different types of relationships. And since everything is in the structure and is not duplicated, constraining the data is simply a matter of limiting the search to only those records that contain the values you want isolated and analyzed.

Focus

Before querying a data structure (database or Triadic Continuum) we generally have a goal in mind. The regional manager for the furniture chain where Bill and Tom work may want to know how many sofas were sold in Pennsylvania, who the best salesperson in the Mid-Atlantic States is, or how much furniture was sold overall in New Jersey and Pennsylvania. All of these are goals. Goals are also known as the "subject of interest" or the "focus," and may be used interchangeably when discussing the Triadic Continuum.

Most often we use the word "focus" and define it as a variable value (a value that can change) that is the subject of interest, usually within a context defined by a set of constraints. While that may sound a bit daunting, a focus is simply the goal you have in mind before constraining data. You really can't constrain data until you know what your goal is. Not until the furniture chain's regional manager has identified that she wants to determine which salesperson has sold the most bedroom suites can she limit the data to the constraints that match her goal. For example, her focus might be to determine if Bill has sold more than Tom in order to determine who wins the "Salesperson of the Month" award.

Context

Before you develop a well thought out goal, you generally have an idea that piques your interest. It may start as a conscious rational thought or as a fuzzy intuitive idea, but it gets you thinking. Either way, before formulating that goal, the idea originates with something that you're thinking about, either consciously or subconsciously.

It's the same with constraining a data set; you need to begin with an idea before formulating a goal. When talking about the Triadic Continuum, we call this pre-goal state "context."

Let's use our regional sales person again. Above we said that she had defined a focus (goal) to identify which salesperson has sold the most furniture. Before she identified this focus, there must have been something that got her thinking about that. It might have been a conversation with Bill, reading a trade journal, or just a fuzzy intuition. Let's say that it was the conversation with Bill. After speaking with him, she wants to know how well the sales teams are doing, or in other words—how well *sales* are going.

Our formal definition says that context is a set of records defined by a set of constraint variable values. Sales are the context since it is the set of records that contain data about the salespersons. Once we have our context, we can determine our focus (the goal) and then identify the values we will need to constrain in order to pursue and attain our focus. In effect the context can also be considered a constraint since it begins to limit the data. In other words, if "Sold" is the context of our inquiry, we first constrain all of the data for "Sold" and then further constrain the data by salespersons and Pennsylvania in order to attain our goal of learning how much each salesperson sold in Pennsylvania. The next figure shows this as a Venn diagram.

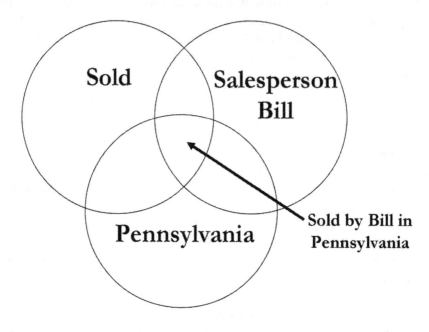

Figure 6–6

The Interplay of Context, Constraint, and Focus

In the realm of the computer and databases, the process of finding answers to questions using the Triadic Continuum is a process of constraining a data set. The first thing that is done is to set the constraint of the query. For example, the context of the Bill and Tom furniture store data might be "Sold," which in effect would constrain the data to only those records that contain nodes associated with the "Sold" Result node, leaving out all of the nodes associated with (connected by dotted lines to) the "Trial" Result node. However, if you want to know what is sold versus what is on trial, the context of the same data set would be all records. So, in order to begin, the context must be selected. It's then a matter of setting the focus, which in effect constrains the data again, say to only those nodes that are associated with "Bill" within the context of "Sold." The process and the interplay of these three concepts—context, constraint, and focus—are intricately entwined in setting context, defining focus, which then constrains the data. This process can be viewed as continuing back and forth until an answer is found—once the context is set, the focus constrains the data, which gives a more focused context from which a new focus constrains a smaller set of data, until finally an answer to a query is realized and thus answered.

Solid and Dotted Lines

Before moving on to relationships, let's talk briefly about the relationship between the solid and dotted lines and context, constraint, and focus. As mentioned earlier, Mazzagatti originally used the solid and dotted lines to make it easier for her to see what was connected to what within the Triadic Continuum. Over time she began to realize that the solid lines represented common two-dimensional tabular data, but that the dotted lines represented something not easily seen in tabular data—relationships. The serendipitous use of dotted lines opened a whole area of thought for Mazzagatti, which led to most of her discoveries of the power of the Triadic Continuum.

Looked at a different way, the solid and dotted lines have a role to play in understanding the interplay among context, constraint, and focus. Within a computer running the Triadic Continuum software, when a context is set, say for example "How many items is Bill selling?" the Result node for "Bill" is found and the dotted line (AsResult connexion) is traced upward to those nodes associated with the Bill. For example, referring back to Figure 6–5, if we trace backward along the dotted line beginning at the "Bill" root node (40), we find one associated "Bill" node (45) with three paths: the Bill_Tuesday_Sofa path (path 50), the Bill_Monday_Table path (path 55), and the Bill_Monday_Sofa path (path 60). Don't forget though that these three paths actually represent six records as indicated by the counter associated with the Bill node.

Therefore, by following the dotted line we begin the process of defining the context, and by having the context we begin to constrain the data to only those paths that contain this associated node. Just to make sure you're with me, I need to remind you that Mazzagatti defines a path as all of the nodes leading backward along a line from an EOT (end product) node to the BOT node.

We further constrain the data by focusing on the number of "Sold" items associated with Bill. Since we're trying to determine how many items Bill is selling, we need to focus on the "Sold" nodes within the context of Bill, so we look at the Result node for "Sold" and trace its dotted lines back to the nodes associated with "Sold," but only those paths that also contain "Bill." Therefore, tracing the dotted lines provides focus (Sold) for the context (Bill). Finally, by determining that there are two nodes associated with the focus "Sold" within the context of "Bill" we constrain the data to only those nodes. We then add up the count in each of those two nodes for a total of five (four in one node and one in another) sold transactions in two days (Monday and Tuesday). Notice that we didn't count the other record leading from Bill (Bill_Monday_Sofa_Trial_PA) because it contains a "Trial" node. We aren't focusing on items on trial; we're focusing on items sold. Notice also that we didn't count the other "Sold" node in the structure because it is associated with Tom. From all of this we determine that Bill sold five items out of the six records associated with him. For Mondays and Tuesdays, Bill has made a sale 83% of the time.

Another way to visualize the interplay of context, focus, and constraint is to think of the structure as a series of electrical circuits. You may remember as a child the science fair or scouting project that used wires and flashlight bulbs to explain and demonstrate how an electrical circuit worked. Usually it consisted of a piece of board with bulbs on one side and wires connecting them on the reverse. Sometimes these projects were made into quiz games where a bulb representing an answer would light up if you answered a question correctly. Each of these projects or games uses wires, batteries, switches, and bulbs to explain how electrical circuits work. For the following example, think of a Result node as an on/off switch, the subcomponent nodes as light bulbs and the solid and dotted connexions as wires connecting the switches to the bulbs. Let's imagine that these wires, which carry the electrical charge to the bulb, are similar to fiber optical cables. When a switch is turned on, the electrical charge passes along the length of the wire/cable to the bulb at the end of the circuit. Because it's an optical cable assume that we can see that it has been activated by it glowing or changing color. And, by the way, for now don't worry about what or where the battery is.

Look at the next figure as you read the following. Now assume that the context is again set to how well Bill is doing at selling furniture. This context sets the Result node "Bill" switch (01) to "on," which causes a charge to travel up the wire/cable to the light bulb (02). Because the bulb (02) is part of a larger circuit, the charge travels along the wires/cables that lead from the Bill bulb (02), which causes the three paths to light up (shown as heavy dark lines.)

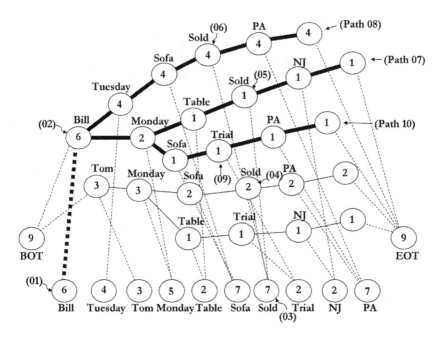

Figure 6–7

Refer now to the next figure. As was done in the previous example, the data is further constrained by focusing on the number of "Sold" items associated with Bill. This is done by turning on the switch for the "Sold" Result node (03), which sends a charge up the three asResult wires/cables to the three bulbs (nodes 04, 05, and 06) connected to that switch.

Because bulb (04) isn't a part of the context, it stays dim even though it is associated with a "Sold" node.

Because paths (07) and (08) are a part of the context circuit (items associated with "Bill" and "Sold"), they stay lit. And, as shown in the next figure, path (10) goes from lit (those currently in context) back to dim, because the focus is not items that are on "Trial" (09) but items "Sold" (nodes 5 and 6) within the overall context of Bill. Notice in the next figure that I've purposely lightened many of the dotted lines so you can see the diagram better.

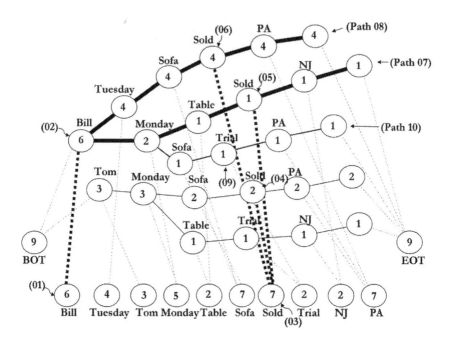

Figure 6–8

In other words, only paths that are within the context and focus of the constrained data are examined when making the calculations necessary to determine how much Bill has sold.

Peirce's Interpretation

I'd like to finish this chapter by using a quote from Peirce's writings to illustrate how Mazzagatti found it necessary to modify some of Peirce's terms to make his language clearer and more relevant to us. It's safe to say that some will think that his words need no modification, that they are clear as is. However, I'll say again as I did in the introduction to this discussion of constraint, focus, and context, that many of us who have read Peirce with an understanding of the Triadic Continuum, find Peirce clearer, more practical, and truly ahead of his time. Peirce wrote the following passage, which is found in his collected papers.

> Reasoning proper begins when I am conscious that the judgment I reach is the effect in my mind of a certain judgment which I had formed before. The judgment which is the cause is called the premise, that which is the effect is called the conclusion. When I am aware that a certain conclusion which I draw is

determined by a certain premise, there are three things which I have more or less clearly in my mind. First, I have a peculiar sense of constraint to believe the conclusion, connected with a sense that that constraint comes from the premise; second, I have a conception that there is a whole class of possible analogous inferences (though I may not be able to define the class) in which a similar constraint would be felt by me; and third I have a present belief that all of these inferences, or at least the great body of them would be true.[15]

Here is the same paragraph with Mazzagatti's terms substituted for what we believe are the corresponding Peirce terms.

Reasoning begins when I am conscious that the judgment I reach is the effect in my mind of a certain judgment which I had formed before. The judgment, which is the cause, is called the **GOAL** that which is the effect is called the conclusion. When I am aware that a certain conclusion, which I draw, is determined by a certain **GOAL**, there are three things, which I have more or less clearly in my mind. First, I have a peculiar sense of **CONSTRAINT** to believe the conclusion, connected with a sense that that constraint comes from the **GOAL**; second, I have a conception that there is a whole class of possible analogous inferences (though I may not be able to define the class) in which a similar **CONSTRAINT** would be felt by me; and third I have a present belief that all of these inferences, or at least the great body of them would be true.

Let me try to make this clearer by using a Bill and Tom furniture store example. In the following table, the left column contains each sentence and/or phase of Mazzagatti's interpretation of Peirce's quote from above. The right column contains a statement that reflects what is taking place within the context of the Bill and Tom scenario.

Mazzagatti Interpretation	*Bill and Tom Example*
Reasoning begins when I am conscious that the judgment I reach is the effect in my mind of a certain judgment which I had formed before.	When looking at the transactional data the manager may make judgments based on her previous knowledge and experience.

Mazzagatti Interpretation	Bill and Tom Example
The judgment, which is the cause, is called the **GOAL** that which is the effect is called the conclusion.	The manager forms a goal. For example, her goal may be formed into the query "How much furniture did Bill sell?" So, her reasoning begins with a conscious goal. In our terminology this goal is called the focus of the manager's query. The focus of the query can be simply stated using only two terms: Bill and Sold.
When I am aware that a certain conclusion, which I draw, is determined by a certain **GOAL**, there are three things, which I have more or less clearly in my mind.	As you will see, the goal of this query (Bill and Sold) determines the answer (conclusion) to the query "How much furniture did Bill sell?"
First, I have a peculiar sense of **CONSTRAINT** to believe the conclusion, connected with a sense that that constraint comes from the **GOAL**;	All of the information found in the furniture store data is constrained by each of the foci. First all of the data is constrained to only those records that contain Bill and then further constrained to all of the Bill records that also contain Sold. Based on this, the conclusion reached is five—Bill has sold five transactions.
second, I have a conception that there is a whole class of possible analogous inferences (though I may not be able to define the class) in which a similar **CONSTRAINT** would be felt by me;	If we look at the data in the furniture store database we realize that there are many other classes of analogous inferences that might be made. For example, one might ask how many Trial transactions Bill had or how many transaction Tom participated in, or even in what state did the most sales occur? All of these are analogous inferences whose class cannot be determined until the constraints are identified.

Mazzagatti Interpretation	Bill and Tom Example
and third I have a present belief that all of these inferences, or at least the great body of them would be true.	Here, both Peirce and Mazzagatti are saying that because every bit of furniture store data has been recorded into the structure of the Triadic Continuum, all of the data are organized in perfect relation to one another and therefore, because of these relationships, all of the inferences about the data must be true. Or, in other words, all analogous inferences are also true, but its not what I'm looking for (my goal) at the moment.

I hope that by now you see why I titled this chapter "Realizing Knowledge." It's because once all of the known data about a given subject—be it furniture store data or a terrorist organization—has been recorded into a K structure; the structure contains all of the relations and associations that exist among the data. Relations and associations are just waiting to be "realized" by establishing a context and formulating a goal, which establishes the focus, which in turn constrains the data in order to reveal a conclusion inherent in the knowledge within the structure. In other words, conclusions aren't made they're realized.

7

Relationships in the Triadic Continuum

A Relationship ... is a fact relative to a number of objects, considered apart from those objects ... Charles Peirce [1]

When speaking of data sets in a field/record universe, the term, "relationship," can be quite specific as well as quite elusive. What exactly does it mean for one piece of data to be related to another? The relationship may be obvious if the relationship is one that inherently exists within a single record, such as the relationship between the last name of a taxpayer and her social security number, but other relationships within different records in a data set may not be so obvious or easily identified. For example, when a potentially effective drug is discovered, the pharmaceutical company performs a series of tests to determine its efficacy and safety. These tests, known as a "clinical trial" may last for years and generally involve what is known as a "double-blind study."

> A double blind study is one in which neither the patient nor the physician knows whether the patient is receiving the treatment of interest or the control treatment. For example, studies of treatments that consist essentially of taking pills are very easy to do double blind—the patient takes one of two pills of identical size, shape, and color, and neither the patient nor the physician needs to know which is which.[2]

Throughout the study, the physician and the patient complete questionnaires about the patient's experience taking the drug. At the end of the clinical trial, these data are entered into a relational database, reviewed, analyzed, and reported to the Food and Drug Administration (FDA). If the trial was long and complex, if there were a large number of patients, or a combination, it's likely that a large amount of data were generated during the study. Analyzing large amounts of data is often a difficult task, and identifying even the most obvious associations isn't always simple; let alone more difficult to identify relationships, such as an interaction between the test medication and a dietary supplement the patient may have taken, the affect of some other disease or condition the patient may have on the action of the drug, or affect of the patient's unique genetic make-up on the metabolism of the drug.

Those employed to analyze relational databases often find it difficult to uncover more than the most obvious relationships. For example, when attempting to discover relationships, an analyst knows that each record in a database (each row) is alone; there is no easy way to know what (if any) relationship exists between the first row in the database and the 10,000[th] row. And so, because it's often so important to discover relationships in data, database programmers have invented and built tools and methods to search for the inherent and tacit relationships in the data.

> In the database world, a relationship is a link that exists between two objects, mainly tables, so that data can flow from one object to another. A relationship can do even more than that: it can be used to check the accuracy of information from one object to another; it can be used to update the information in one object when related information in another object has been changed.[3]

Types of Relationships

Those working in data modeling and data mining, categorize the types of relationships that they suggest exist within data in a database. And, as with any complex topic such as this, one can find numerous books and articles that explain the "hows" and "whys" of database relationships. In these books, the experts, besides having categorized and defined the types of relationships, have also identified and documented the attributes, characteristics, and rules associated with each type of relationship. It's not my purpose here to debate the different rules and definitions; I accept the fact that these conventions have been developed over time in order to understand and work with the format, organization, and access method of the data structure they are using. My purpose here is to show the superiority of the "knowledge structure" of the Triadic Continuum in comparison to older "data structures." So, in the following discussion, I use a common categorization scheme that is not uncommon to most data modelers and data miners.

Some data analysts talk about the categories of relationships as being four-fold: specific, non-specific, categorization, and recursive.

> A specific relationship or a "parent-child" relationship is an association or connection between entities in which each instance of one entity—the parent entity—is associated with zero, one or more instances of a second entity—the child entity.
>
> A non-specific relationship, also referred to as a "many-to-many" relationship," is an association between two entities in which each instance of the first entity is associated with zero, one, or many instances of the second entity.
>
> A Categorization Relationship is used to represent structures in which an entity is a "type" (category) of another entity. A categorization relationship is a relationship between one entity, referred to as the "generic entity," and another entity, referred to as "category entity." Each instance of the category entity represents the same real-world thing as its associated instance in the generic entity.
>
> A Recursive Relationship is where an entity has a relationship to itself.[4]

Other data analysts further divide these associations into sub-categories of relationships based on other attributes and values that the relationships may be deemed to have. For example, relationships may be further described by the direction of the relationship, i.e., which entity is deemed the parent and which the child. Then, in order to analyze the stored data, programmers must develop complex software to look for the relationships (associations, attributes, and values) within the data, which one might consider to be "structured," since only those relationships that have been formally identified may be found.

And still other data analysts categorize relationships by the type of software that has been engineered to seek out relationships within a data structure. There are those who identify four types of relationships: classes, clusters, associations, and sequential patterns.[5]

However, no matter which way you categorize relationships; they are generally defined as an association between two entities. And, because associations are limited by the type, format, and organization of the specific data structure, some relationships that may actually exist in the data, but are not associated by the structured and formal associations defined above, will never be found in a traditional structure.

As I have attempted to explain in the earlier chapters, the structure of the Triadic Continuum makes it uniquely different from that of traditional data structures. And, it is the differences that not only make finding simple relationships easier and quicker, but also makes seeking and finding the more complex relationships possible.

The remainder of this chapter talks more about the Triadic Continuum and how relationships are "realized." For the discussion that follows, I talk about simple and complex relationships. By "simple" I mean those relationships and information that are relatively easy to find in traditional databases with commonly available analytical software tools and methods, but by comparison to finding the same entities in a Triadic Continuum are primitive. And by "complex," I mean those that illustrate the four categories of relationships: associations, sequential patterns, clusters, and classification.

Simple Relationships

The following relationships are examples that can be accomplished within a traditional database or other type of data structure. Because designers and programmers have been creating databases for close to 50 years, they've gotten good at working around the inherent shortcomings of the data structure. They've also modified the original design and added methods and enhancements like indexes and arrays to make them more efficient. They've invented multi-dimensional cubes in order to locate more complex relationships in two-dimensional data. And while this seems like a major advancement over a simpler single-dimensional data structure, cubes are really nothing more then multi two-dimensional tables fitted together in a faux three-dimensional package. And while this works to a degree, the cost in manpower and time to construct these tools is clearly and recognizably substantial.

It is not my intent to minimize the effort of the computer scientists that pioneered and still work in this area; they should be praised for their intellectual prowess and ingenuity in making the database as powerful as it is. However, like DVD and CD replacing VCR and vinyl records, new inventions, and more importantly new paradigms, eventually either prove their superiority over the old or vanish. We believe that in time the power of the Triadic Continuum will be recognized as superior to that of the database, not because it is new, but because it can find complex, as well as simple relationships faster and more efficiently than technologies like cubes and neural networks.

All of this power comes from the fact that, as said earlier in the chapter, everything is in the structure of the Triadic Continuum; all of the simple and complex relationships are there, as a naturally occurring outcome of the data itself. The relationships are there just waiting for someone to ask the right question—there's no need to re-program or do anything but ask the right question.

The following examples show how the Triadic Continuum can find simple relationships, ones that can also be accomplished within a traditional database or other types of data structures, but more quickly and efficiently.

Realizing Distinct Records

The first example of a simple relationship that can be realized using a Triadic Continuum is in finding distinct records. A distinct record is the number of specific records that were created from all of the data input into the Triadic Continuum. To find the total number of distinct records you simply count each path leading from the EOT node. For example, in the next figure, there are five paths leading from the EOT node, which means there are five *distinct* records out of the original nine data records read into the structure.

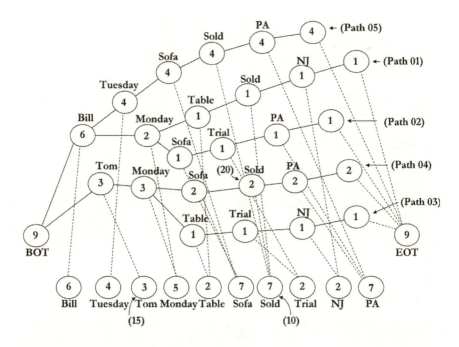

Figure 7–1

Realizing Unique Records

Realizing unique records is the second example of a simple relationship that can be found using a Triadic Continuum. Unique records are those that occur only once in the structure. To find records that are unique, you begin at an End of Thought node, which in actuality represents the end of a record. As you look at the last diagram, trace backward from the EOT node the paths to locate nodes that have a count of one (1). A node with a count of "1" is unique; it only occurred once in the set of data records that were input and built into a Triadic Continuum. For example, starting at EOT and traversing up the five pathways leading from it, you see that there are three nodes with a count of one. Three nodes with a count of one indicate that there are three unique records: BOT-Bill-Monday-Table-Sold-NJ-EOT (path 01), BOT-Bill-Monday-Sofa-Trial-PA-EOT (path 02), and BOT-Tom-Monday-Table-Trial-NJ-EOT (path 03). To accomplish this, other than following the first dotted line from EOT to the end product nodes, you only traversed solid Case lines back along the Case path (solid lines) back to BOT.

We consider finding unique records an example of a simple relationship because it's something that can easily be found in a relational database or similar data structure. The solid lines simply represent a single record in a simple two-dimensional table, albeit structured in a fairly unique way. But, the data represented by the nodes is really nothing more than column and row data, and the solid line represents a simple two-dimensional look at this field/record data.

Realizing Duplicated Records

The third example of locating simple relationships within the structure of the Triadic Continuum deals with duplicated data. In the previous figure there are two records that are duplicated: BOT-Tom-Monday-Sofa-Sold-PA-EOT (path 04), with a count of two in the End Product node leading up from the EOT and BOT-Bill-Tuesday-Sofa-Sold-PA-EOT (path 05), with a count of four records. Counts higher than one represent records that are duplicated. Again, an extremely simple search for end product nodes with counts higher than "1" uncover duplicates in the structure.

Realizing Information Using Counters

To find out some specific piece of information, say for example how many items in the data were sold, one simply has to go to the Result node "Sold" and look at its counter. You may remember from the last chapter that "counters" were defined as a feature added by Mazzagatti to keep track of the number of times each specific particle is experienced. In Figure 7–1, the Sold Result node (10) has a count of seven. That means that by looking at only one node, one can determine the total number of items designated as sold in the entire structure. Unlike traditional databases, in a Triadic Continuum this is a single step process. The computer doesn't have to traverse each record keeping a count of how many sold items there are; it's simply a matter of going to a single Result node and looking at its counter.

Realizing Information by Intersecting Paths

Another way to realize a specific piece of information is to determine the count at two intersecting paths. For example, to find how many items Tom sold, you begin at the Sold Result node (10) and the Tom result node (15) and trace a path to the node that connects these two nodes. Again, using Figure 7–1, the count of that node (20) is two, or in other words, Tom sold two items.

Realizing Less Obvious Information

One less obvious example is if you're trying to easily find out who sold the most items in your database. Instead of searching all of the records for all of the salespersons and adding up each by total number of sales, with a Triadic Continuum, it's just a matter of starting at the Result node for "Sold" (10) and tracing the Result connexions. Again using the Bill and Tom example, there are three paths that contain "Sold": one path to BOT-Bill-Tuesday-Sofa-Sold, with a count of four, one path to BOT-Bill-Monday-Table-Sold, with a count of one, and one path to BOT-Tom-Monday-Sofa-Sold, with a count of two. The first two paths include nodes that point to Bill and the counters indicate that Bill sold a total of four items. The third path leads to Tom and the counter indicates that he sold two items. Therefore, Bill sold more than Tom.

I realize that the above examples may seem simplistic, but that's only because we're talking about a structure with only nine records. It's not difficult to see the value of searching for a single "Sold" Result node in a structure made up of thousands of nodes constructed from hundreds of thousands of transaction data records. The largest database today (circa 2006) may be upward of 100 terabytes in size. Just for comparison, today's PC hard drive may hold approximately 500 gigabytes of data, which is about ½ a terabyte (1000 gigabytes = 1 terabyte).[6] So, a 100-terabyte database is equal to the amount of data that will fit on roughly 200 PC hard drives—that's a lot of data.

In most databases, all data records for transactions, such as sold, must be searched individually in order to calculate the total number of "sold" transactions. So, if it's a large terabyte-sized database, the task isn't simple. However, searching for a single "Sold" Result node in a Triadic Continuum *is* simple. And, it doesn't matter if there are nine "Sold" records or 900 million; all "Sold" records will be accessed from a single "Sold" Result node. And, while that in itself is impressive, it is the nature of the three-dimensionality of the Triadic Continuum where the power and uniqueness of the structure is truly in evidence.

Complex Relationships

As the term implies, complex relationships are more involved than the simple ones explained above. In general, the discovery of complex data relationships takes much more persistent investigation than the more simple and obvious relationships.

In the following chapters I'll talk about four different categories of complex relationships as categorized by one author in a paper on data mining. I just as easily could have decided to use someone else's groupings, but the following four types—classes, associations, sequential patterns, and clusters—work well in explaining more complex relationships. In data mining, "generally, any of the four types of relationships are sought

Classes: Stored data is used to locate data in predetermined groups.

Associations: Data can be mined to identify associations. An example in the retail business might be where historic data is used to "identify that customers who purchase the *Gladiator* DVD and the *Patriot* DVD also purchase the *Braveheart* DVD." [7]

Sequential patterns: Data is mined to anticipate behavior patterns and trends. For example, an outdoor equipment retailer could predict the likelihood of a backpack being purchased based on a consumer's purchase of sleeping bags and hiking shoes.

Clusters: Data items are grouped according to logical relationships or consumer preferences. For example, data can be mined to identify market segments or consumer affinities. [8]

As I talk about each of these relationships in the following chapters, I'll define them and then provide an example of how they are realized using the Triadic Continuum. It's also important to understand that as I talk about these relationships, they may sound similar to one another. That's perfectly normal. For one thing, I've already defined "relationship" as an association between two or more entities, and, because of this, some of the terminology may overlap and may even be used interchangeably. For example, in the next chapter, I talk about classifying information. One offshoot of classification, or grouping, is that often things group in clusters; and clusters are another type of relationship. So, in some sense classification may be considered a type of cluster. There are many more examples that show how interrelated the types of relationships are, but if you'll be flexible, I'll try to draw a finer line between each of the types of relationships. What's more important than the fact that the definition of relationships may overlap, is the fact that by using the Triadic Continuum you can easily and quickly find simple and complex relationships, as well as other previously unknown relationships that may actually exist in data, but because of more traditional data structures is difficult or impossible to see. Let's begin with classification and then continue on to patterns in time, associations, and finally end with clusters.

8

Classification

All classification, whether artificial or natural, is the arrangement of objects according to ideas. A natural classification is the arrangement of them according to those ideas from which their existence results. Charles Peirce[1]

At first glance, the meaning of the word "classification" may seem quite clear. To many of us, the term classification brings back memories of high school biology, where it is recognized as the process of organizing living things into categories, such as Kingdom, Genus, and species. This organization is based on the ideas of 18th century Swedish botanist Carolus Linnaeus, who proposed a taxonomic scheme that dominated biological classification until quite recently. But, the concept of "classification" has much more meaning than its use with animals and plants suggests. Two thousand years ago the Greek philosopher and scientist Aristotle not only proposed a scheme for classifying plants and animals, but is also credited with classifying politics, mathematics, government, as well as the more challenging concepts of human morals and virtues.

If we look at the concept of classification in terms of modern cognitive science, classification can mean how we recognize, understand, and organize the objects in our environment as well as how we categorize the ideas and thoughts in our own mind. But why is this important? It may simply be that we, as a species, have a need to bring order to an ever-changing chaotic world by grouping things and ideas into a scheme that makes sense to each of us. However, the idea that we create our own classification of the world, brings with it two related issues that illustrate the difference between "classification" as it is seen today and how it can be viewed with a knowledge of the structure of the Triadic Continuum—that of *classifier* and *objectivity*. Let me explain.

As I understand it, the "aim of every classification is *to establish* order in things and in thought."[2] With that in mind, the phrase "to establish" suggests that someone, the author of the scheme, commonly called the "classifier," creates the classification. Most definitions of the term classification imply that there is this classifier who designs the classification scheme based on his or her observations and experiences. And, if you have ever tried to agree with someone whether a tomato is a fruit or a vegetable, you'll understand that individuals often perceive and categorize the same object or event in startlingly different ways.

The second issue deals with the fact that a classification scheme, by its very nature is based on the observations, ideas, and knowledge of the classifier, with either implicit or tacit agreement of those who accept its worth. Some would say that a classification scheme "may appear to be natural and obvious to those who accept it, but in reality is an invention or artifact"[3] of a particular classifier. The validity of a classification scheme often relies on personal scientific opinion as much as hard empirical evidence. As well, and without impugning the knowledge, skill, and ethics of any classifier who has come before, it's recognized and understood that the objectivity of the classifier can play a major role in how something is classified. Take for instance the following paragraph, written by a molecular geneticist in a paper on the classification of an African amphibian:

> Unfortunately, taxonomists do not always agree as to the proper distribution of groups of animals. Disagreement can arise because of a number of factors. These include a changing evaluation of the relationships between groups, improvement in the techniques or measurements that are being used, a reassessment of the value of various characteristics, and additional data that reduces the significance of previous studies.[4]

As the author points out, one of the reasons that disagreements arise is because of a "changing evaluation of the relationships between groups."[5] We can take this to mean that different classifiers may evaluate the same data in different ways depending on their conscious interpretation of the data or on unconscious biases based on previous experiences. Again, I'm not suggesting that any classifier, scientist or lay person ever tries to group something into a class other than where it should rightfully be, but I am suggesting that the act of classification is done by humans, and like most human endeavors may be influenced by biases and simple differences of opinions.

In trying to alleviate the subjectivity of classifiers those who practice the scientific method attempt to bring increasing levels of quantification to the sciences. In sciences like physics, chemistry and biology, which use quantifiable methods, the probability of inaccurate classification becomes more remote every day. For example, when scientific classification and taxonomy were first established, the classification of plants and animals was based on morphology, physiology, and the fossil record of living things. However, in modern biology, chemistry and molecular phylogenetics use strenuously quantifiable methods and procedures to help resolve how living things are categorized—"it's a bird because it has wings and a beak"[6] has been replaced with the fact that it's a bird because of its DNA and protein sequences.

In the more theoretical sciences and in fields such as business, economics, and finance, classification may seem more subjective because the results are a product of a conscious mental act that takes whatever evidence there is and postulates a classification scheme. But as explained by Judith Rosen, daughter of the late theoretical biologist Robert Rosen, this mental act

> takes the form of "If *this,* then there must also be *that* ... "and "In order for *this* to be, there must also have been *that.*" So, far from being mere speculation, theoretical science involves a great deal of knowledge and an ability to connect incomplete glimpses of evidence into a logically sound ... pattern which can then be tested ... [7]

Still, no matter how objective and knowledgeable the classifier, how quantifiable the methodology and results, or how logically the criteria were postulated, classification, by its very nature is often more personal and subjective than the classifier wants or believes it to be.

> The very fact that classification appeals to logical criteria which may possibly be subjective or objective in nature gives us an initial idea of the obstacles confronting the classifier, difficulties scarcely encountered in the preparation of a catalogue, properly so called. Consequently, a well conducted effort ... may be valuable in leading us to discover the connections and analogies existing among the different fields of knowledge at a given time ..."[8]

The preceding quote highlights the difficulty that the "classifier" encounters when preparing a truly objective classification scheme as she endeavors to determine subjective criterion based on objective observations. However, there's an idea embedded in the quote that I believe is more relevant to our discussion of the Triadic Continuum, and that is the idea that if the classifier conducts an exemplary analysis of thought and ideas, she may discover the "*connections and analogies*" (the relationships) that exist among the knowledge (italics added).

The idea that connections and analogies exist within all of the information the classifier has at her disposal brings us back to our discussion earlier in this chapter on relationships that exist within data. As the author of the previous quote suggests, a well-conducted effort at preparing a classification is valuable in helping the classifier to discover the relationships that exist within the data. However, as has been explained, relationships occur naturally in the structure of the Triadic Continuum—the connections between and among the relationships are naturally formed from the data as the structure is built; there is no need, nor any value for an external classifier to impose an unnatural categorization upon the data—the classification is there already, waiting for someone to recognize it for what it is. In other words, in the Triadic Continuum, classification is not imposed *on the information*; classification is derived *from within the information*.

The idea that classification comes out of the structure, not out of the classifier's mind became apparent to Mazzagatti as she studied the implications of the three-dimensionality of the structure and realized the meaning of the dotted and solid lines. She quickly understood that this formed the basis of what Peirce called the "natural classes."

If one looks at the intellectual life of Charles Peirce, a major part of it was spent thinking and writing about the nature of classification. He seems to be compelled toward a need to classify the sciences and conjecture grandly upon categorizations of all known knowledge. It's been suggested by learning theorists that there are two fundamental orientations in learning: "splitters, who tend to analyze information logically and break it down into smaller parts, and lumpers, who tend to watch for patterns and relationships between the parts."[9] Peirce seems to be one of those individuals who was inclined toward both orientations; quite possibly this is one of the abilities of his genius. However, the difficulty he had throughout his life moving from the theoretical "big picture" to actually completing a final draft of his philosophy, may have been as much about his own learning orientation as it was about the health and welfare of he and his wife. In any case, Peirce seems to have been driven by the need to create a formal philosophy, a classification scheme of "the fundamental categories of thought."[10] And, like "lumpers" who's "thinking process begins with a mental image ... and then moves to the specifics if necessary,"[11] Peirce spent much of his life in the process of constructing this framework but seemed thwarted in his attempt to complete it.

However, the rudiments of Peirce's philosophy can be seen in a paper written in 1867 called "On a New List of Categories." This paper was "The culmination of a ten-year effort and the keystone of Peirce's system of philosophy, it argues for a new post-Kantian set of categories (or universal conceptions) by demonstrating that they are required for the unification of experience."[12] Peirce became convinced that formal logic depended on these categories and that they "really did and must exist."[13] With knowledge of the structure of the Triadic Continuum it might be said that Peirce would have been comfortable saying that predicate logic is one view of the structure, while higher order logic represents a different view of the structure.

Almost 20 years later he wrote "One, Two, Three: Fundamental Categories of Thought and of Nature," in which he "introduced his strategy of deriving categories from the mathematics of logic."[14] He planned to expand this manuscript into a book, but instead, it was incorporated into the first chapter of "A Guess at the Riddle." Reading the draft outline for "A Guess at the Riddle,"[15] one gets the sense that this was to be his magnum opus, and would boldly define the categories of his philosophy. While many of the ideas that were fundamental to understanding his philosophy were published in a series of articles in *The Monist*,[16] the magnum opus was never written.

The drafts and notes for the "Guess" book, as well as the published articles show that he planned to classify all of the sciences within his three theoretical categories in a logical arrangement of topics. However, it appears that he had no guiding principle to explain how the topics were arranged, simply suggesting that the work would be completed, in his own words, in a "follow my leader"[17] approach as work was completed in one topic to another, starting with a discussion of his categories themselves. As a planned outline for his opus, the detailed outline is bold in scope. The book was to open with a discussion of his belief in the trichotomy of logical ideas as he had explained in "One, Two, Three: Kantian Categories." Peirce remarks in the opening outline of Chapter 1, "Trichotomy," that

In fact, I make so much use of the threefold divisions in my speculations, that it seems best to commence by making a slight preliminary study of the conceptions upon which all such divisions must rest.[18]

The second chapter was to cover the importance of the triad in reasoning. Chapter 3 was to explain how his triadic approach could be used to explain metaphysics, the philosophy of the mind. No less bold were Chapters 4–9, which were to cover the triadic nature of psychology, physiology, biology, physics, sociology, and theology respectively.

It seems that Peirce regarded his speculations as to the nature of philosophy as not only bold, but monumental. As Peirce scholar Nathan Hauser writes "Sometime in 1885, it occurred to Peirce that he may have found the key to the secret of the universe, and he wrote to William James on 20 October"[19]

I have something very vast now … It is … an attempt to explain the laws of nature, to show their general characteristics and to trace them to their origin & predict new laws by the laws of the laws of nature."[20]

Hauser continues by mentioning "it remained for him to work the details and consequences of this grand hypothesis into a full-fledged theory."[21] But, the closest Peirce ever came to formalizing his grand framework seems to have been in his outline and manuscripts in preparation for "A Guess at the Riddle." Less than five years before his death, he wrote to English philosopher Victoria Lady Welby

The truth is that there are great obstacles to my writing. In the first place I am 70 years old and perceive that my powers of mind are beginning to fail, and I feel that it is my most sacred of all duties to write that book which shall show that many powerful minds have held views apparently the most antipodal upon the subjects of the highest concern to all men, merely because they have all alike missed that point of view which would have reconciled them all in one truth, and which will incidentally show any intelligent person how to think in such a way as to reach the truth expeditiously.[22]

A few sentences later in the same letter Peirce says, "… I feel that I am in possession of truth which must be put into writing before my powers quite fail. This haunts me constantly …"[23]

As another Peirce scholar so succinctly puts it, "his mature philosophy never made its way intact out of the universe of ideas and onto paper."[24] However, while he may not have given us his penultimate treatise with all of the threads neatly wrapped up, he did leave us with a number of interesting thoughts, theories, and ideas related to classification.

As I mentioned in Chapter 1, while many people believe Peirce to be primarily a philosopher, he looked at all interesting questions through the eyes of a scientist. So it isn't unrealistic to believe that he did the same with the concept of classification. In writing about the classification of the sciences he explains that

> We should not begin the execution of the task until we have well considered, first, what classification is; and secondly, what science is ... [25]

> The first question then, that it seems well to consider (remembering that classification is one of the topics of logic to be dealt with more scientifically in its proper place, and that I can here only skim the surface of it) is, What is meant by a true and natural class? A great many logicians say there is no such thing; and, what is strange, even many students of taxonomic sciences not only follow this opinion, but allow it a great part in determining the conclusions of botany and zoology. The cause of their holding this opinion has two factors; first, that they attach a metaphysical signification to the term natural or real class, and secondly, that they have embraced a system of metaphysics which allows them to believe in no such thing as that which they have defined a real or natural class to be.[26]

In this passage Peirce explicitly calls out the fact that he believes that classification is a subject that can be addressed scientifically. He also states that there are indeed natural classes and seems surprised that some logicians and taxonomists believe that natural classes do not actually exist. He continues by vigorously explaining that their disbelief lies in their certainty that the question of natural classes is metaphysically unanswerable to scientific observation, experimentation, or analysis.

Kelly Parker writes that Peirce believed that "the key concept for any classification is the *natural class*."[27] Peirce says

> A class, of course, is the total of whatever objects there may be in the universe which are of a certain description. What if we try taking the term "natural," or "real, class" to mean a class of which all the members owe their existence as members of the class to a common final cause?[28]

By "natural class" I believe Peirce meant a categorization not based on the subjective interpretation of a classifier, but on the general values, attributes, and meaning naturally associated with any specific object or idea. In his writing on classification Peirce calls these general values the object's "final cause," by which he means the general purpose exhibited by all members of the class—"A thing belongs to a natural class by virtue of its realizing the final cause as all the members of that class."[29] Peirce uses an example of a gas lamp to explain final cause and natural class, which Parker explains by saying, "Lamps of whatever variety, for example, belong to the class of lamps because they are all designed to provide illumination."[30] This may seem to be obvious when the discussion is about man-made objects, such as lights; but final cause is more difficult to discern in natural objects, such as in the classification of plants and animals. "Peirce recognized that we cannot usually discern the final cause that all its members all realize. Nonetheless, he held that the same principle applies"[31] to natural objects as it does to man-made objects and ideas.

In his book *The Continuity of Peirce,* Kelly Parker, makes three perceptive arguments about classification that I need to expand on through the prism of the Triadic Continuum:

- Classification is not conscious
- Classification is uncertain
- Classification is not a matter of definition

Classification Is Not Conscious

When I say that classification is not conscious I mean that the classifier has nothing to do with the establishment of a true natural class as meant by Charles Peirce. She may identify the common characteristics and features of a group of objects or living things and from that define a classification scheme; however, she has not consciously identified the final cause, even though it might seem so. As Parker writes, "A final cause is not necessarily a conscious purpose, though that is the form most familiar to us.[32] In fact, because of our knowledge of the Triadic Continuum, we now know that all attempts at conscious classification, no matter how accurate and scientifically qualitative or quantitative they are will never be as accurate as the categories that are naturally formed as a result of the building of the structure of the Triadic Continuum.

Classification Is Uncertain

In our earlier discussion on the objectivity of the classifier I suggested that there is an inherent uncertainty to classification, which I suggested might be due to a number of factors including, as I mentioned, unconscious bias and differences of opinion. Parker believes that Peirce might agree when he paraphrases him by writing, "In many cases an object exhibits features characteristic of more than one class. Unless we have more information (of the object's history, for example) it may be impossible for us to be sure what its primary purpose is."[33] However, not having knowledge of the Triadic Continuum, Parker writes

> All we can do in setting out to classify objects is to look for their apparent sim-ilarities and try to identify as best we can the final cause that similar objects fulfill. Objects that share a common final cause, and hence exhibit similar fea-tures, are included in the same natural class. Clearly, in many cases the final cause will be unknown, and mere similarity of objects' features does not allow us to describe natural classes. It is an inconvenient fact of nature that every-thing exhibits *some* similarities to anything else we may choose. Lacking addi-tional information, we have no way to tell which ones are "important" characteristics of an object, for purposes of classification.[34]

Using the Triadic Continuum it is possible to build a structure based on all of the known relevant data about an object, which will show the natural classes that naturally cluster together in the structure. For example, a Triadic Continuum could be built using data about animals with a similar physical appearance to see if they are naturally grouped together or to build a structure with all the financial and organizational data about a number of companies, to discover, for example which traits are similar within a natural group of "successful" companies.

Classification Is Not a Matter of Definition

When we create a classification scheme, for example, a taxonomic tree, we are forced to start at the bottom of the scheme "with a sampling of particular objects that we *suppose* might belong together, and look for shared qualities,"[35] instead of starting at the top "with a sure identification of the final cause that brings a broad class of objects into existence." But discovering the final cause of natural objects isn't a simple task and so we create definitions of the classes that we build from the bottom up. Again, with the Triadic Continuum this is done by the structure, and the structure does not define the classes so much as discover the natural classes that exist.

I need to make one final point before showing examples of how the Triadic Continuum can be used in practical application of classification, and that is the notion of the final achievement of natural class. What I mean by this is that, in theory, a classification is never complete so long as there are still facts to learn about the object or idea. Contemporary philosophers hold different views on this, but in a paper on Peirce's idea of natural classes, Menno Hulswit writing about another philosopher's interpretation of Peirce's natural classes says that "If science were to continue long enough, it would yield true classifications and true laws of nature, that is to say, classifications and laws"[36] "from which the local and idiosyncratic, the unreal, had been eliminated"[37]

Theoretically, as more and more bits of data are discovered about, for example, the interactions surrounding and encompassing a living thing or the micro and macro environments of the financial universe, and input into the Triadic Continuum, the more the structure will change and grow, and the more complete the classification will become. And only then, as we approach the totality of knowledge about something will the true natural class emerge. As Peirce writes, "A class, of course, is the total of whatever objects there may be in the universe which are of a certain description."[38] However, this final universal totality is predicated on the discovery of all knowledge that there is to know about a given subject; whether or not that is possible is, and will continue to be a question for philosophers and scientists to answer.

Classification and the Triadic Continuum

So far, I've explained what I think Peirce and some of those who study his works believe he meant by classification. In the following section I use two examples to illustrate how Peirce's meaning of classification, natural classes, and final cause can be adapted, through the use of the Triadic Continuum into practical application.

Mazzagatti and those who work on the computer implementation of the Triadic Continuum define classification as a systematic arrangement of objects (of any type) into groups or categories according to a set of established criteria. What they mean by this is that once data is learned into the Triadic Continuum; there exist groupings that are predetermined by the fact that the relationships that exist between the data are discovered once learned into the structure. There may actually be relationships that exist within the data that are difficult or impossible for even experts in the subject matter to see, even though these experts may have spent a career observing, experimenting, studying, and analyzing the data.

Finding classes in stored data is extremely important in the sciences, but it can be just as useful and important in other fields as well. "For example, a restaurant chain could mine customer purchase data to determine when customers visit and what they typically order. This information could be used to increase traffic by having daily specials."[39] What they would be doing is mining the data to try and discover the natural classifications that exist, for example looking for a grouping of times and then associated groupings of what items are ordered. This is something that can be done today; however, it takes time and resources. With the Triadic Continuum this is simply a matter of inputting all of the data and asking the questions. It really is that easy. That's why the following examples are meant to show how practical the Triadic Continuum is in finding predetermined groups in everyday business data.

Contexted Classification

When business data is entered into a Triadic Continuum, the three-dimensional nature of the structure allows analysts to quickly see the natural classes that exist and which can be used to make business decisions. For example, the minute the business data is entered into a Triadic Continuum, an analysis can be performed to create a classification that could be used to categorize bank loan applications as either safe or risky. Currently, there are multiple classification analytics that are used with the Triadic Continuum, such as contexted classification, Bayes classification, and dynamic decision tree, but the following example uses an analytic Mazzagatti calls contexted classification.

Contexted classification is a very specific type of classification that performs a classification only on the information the business analyst identifies. The contexted classification analytic, which searches the structure, limits the data searched to only those fields that the analyst wants to include in the classification. By doing this, the analyst selects to disregard information not considered important or relevant within the "context" of the business problem. The result is a classification that shows the highest probability of each of the fields selected by the analyst. As already mentioned, this type of classification can be used in business to analyze credit risk, sales transactions, and why some customers choose to stay and others leave. The following is an example of an analysis of sales transactions.

In the following scenario I use the same Bill and Tom furniture sales fictional data that I have used in previous examples. This data contains nine records and refers to the number of items sold by individual salespersons in different regions of the country on different days of the week. The following picture is the Triadic Continuum that is produced as a result of the nine furniture store records.

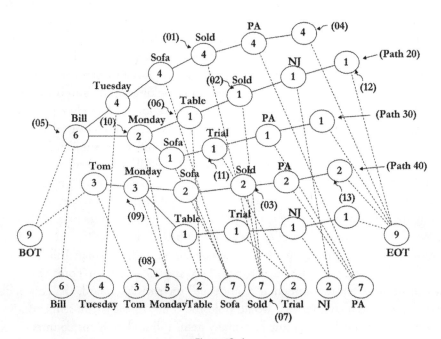

Figure 8–1

In explaining how classification works in the Triadic Continuum, I use two examples. The first will ask which salesperson sold the most furniture and the second will ask which salesperson sold the most furniture on Monday. The first example shows a simple use of classification and counters, as explained in the opening of this chapter, while the second shows how data, which is limited to a specific context, can be classified.

However, before beginning the examples, there's one more thing that you need to understand. Earlier when I explained the types of K nodes that are included in a Triadic Continuum I didn't mention the end node. An end node is the very last K node in a sequence of K nodes. In a computer built Triadic Continuum, the computer program that controls the construction of the data structure adds the end node.

Like other K nodes, each end node contains a counter. However, the end node contains a counter that represents the total number of times the particular sequence is experienced. For example, referring back to the previous diagram, the K node numbered (12) is an end node and contains the number "1," which represents the number of times the sequence Bill_Monday_Table_Sold_NJ was experienced. In other words, there is only one record of Bill selling tables on Monday in New Jersey. The end node counter is important when you're looking for certain types of data. For example, say you're looking for the number of items sold by Bill. If you took the number in the counter for the K node representing Bill (5), you'll see that it contains the number six. This of course refers to the number of records that have been experienced with Bill as the subject. However, it does not represent the number of items sold by Bill. To determine the total number of items Bill sold, the Triadic Continuum's search analytic first begins at elemental K node number (07) representing "Sold." It then traverses backward along the asResult path to the K nodes that are associated with items sold. In this example there are three K nodes associated with sold (K nodes 01, 02, and 03). However, only two of them are also in association with salesman Bill, K node numbers (01) and (02); the other K node (03) is associated with Tom. Since the search begins from the elemental K node and traverses backward, the end node was designed as a counter that would hold the count or the entire sequence. So, in order to accurately determine how many items Bill sold, only the counters in K nodes numbered (01) and (02) are totaled, since they are the K nodes associated with both Bill and Sold.

If all you were looking for were the number of items sold, only one K node (the elemental K node numbered 07) would be needed. But, once you introduce more criteria, such as which salesperson or day of the week, it becomes necessary to use the end nodes. So, with the end nodes in mind, now let's see how classification works in the Triadic Continuum.

Example 1

Determining who sold the most furniture is as simple as locating the K node for all of the items sold, which in the above diagram is identified by the number (07). Noticing the counter in the K node, we see that seven items were sold. To determine who sold the most, we trace the path back along the asResult dotted line to those K nodes that have K nodes associated with sold, which in the diagram are the K nodes numbered (01, 02, and 03). Then, from each K node the asCase path is traversed until the end product node is reached. The number in the counter of each end product node is found. For example, the counter in end product node (04) is 4. Then the Case path is traversed backward from each end product node until a K node associated with Bill or Tom is found. The result of this operation shows that Bill sold 5 items and Tom sold 2. You might be thinking that because the Bill K node (05) has a counter of 6 within it that Bill sold 6 items. However, that's the reason we started by tracing back from the Sold K node and not just look at the Bill or the Tom K node. Had we started by searching back from the Bill K node, we would have first found the Bill K node (05) with the counter 6. By doing that we would have missed the fact that one of Bill's transactions has a "Trial" K node (11) and a trial is not a sold transaction. The same goes for Tom, who also had one trial transaction. Again, as I talked about earlier, this seems like a simplistic example until you understand that this data structure works the same no matter if there are nine records or 9,000,000 records. There's always a single "Sold" K node that always points to only those K nodes that are associated with "Sold" records; there is no need to search non-relevant records.

In this example, the class of "Sold" is found by simply traversing paths whose point of origin is the elemental root K node "Sold" (07). There is no need for a classifier to define what the classification should be; the classification comes out of the structure itself.

Example 2

Now let's look at a contexted classification using the same data, but this time we want to know who sold the most furniture on Monday. In this example we're focusing on the salespersons, but we're limiting the records to only those for items that were sold on Monday. In other words, we're asking for a classification of records that contain the natural classes "Sold" and "Monday," so we purposely constrain (limit) the records to only those associated with "Sold" and "Monday."

We begin by locating the K nodes for "Sold" and "Monday" in the Triadic Continuum shown in the previous figure, which are identified with the numbers (07) and (08). The "Monday" K node contains a count of 5 and the "Sold" K node a count of "7." Because we've already done the first scenario we know that the difference is because of the two "Trail" transactions; but that's not important in this scenario, so let's continue.

What is important, however, is that the count for "Monday" is lower than the count for "Sold." This tells us that because there are less instances of Monday that our search may be quicker than that for "Sold." Therefore, we start with "Monday" and trace back along the asResult dotted lines to those K nodes associated with "Monday." In this example we see that there are two K nodes that are associated with the K node for "Monday," which are identified with the numbers (09) and (10). We next need to determine which of the paths that leads forward from these K nodes contains K nodes associated with "Sold." In this way, we've first limited the K nodes we need to look at to only those associated with Monday and then limited the subset further to only those associated with "Sold" on "Monday." So, the structure is then traversed forward from each of the "Monday" K nodes searching for those K nodes that are associated with "Sold."

What happens in this scenario is that there are actually four paths leading from the two "Monday" subcomponent K nodes (09) and (10). The first path, identified by the label "Path 20," includes "Table" on to a K node associated with "Sold," which is a hit. The second path, labeled "Path 30" stops at the K node "Trial" (11), as does the fourth path. The third path, labeled "Path 40," which also contains a K node associated with "Sold" (03), is also a hit, so both paths 20 and 40 continue to be traversed to the end product node. The end product node, (12) (at the end of Path 20) contains a count of "1" and the end product node number (13) (at the end of Path 40) has a count of "2." Therefore, we know that there are a total of "3" instances of items sold on Monday. However, the question still remains as to who was better at selling on Monday?

Next, the Case paths are traversed back to the K node representing the salespersons, Bill and Tom. The count within the K node representing Bill (05) is "6" and the count within the K node representing Tom is "3," but those counts only reflect the total number of records experienced for both of the salesman. The way to determine who sold the most items has already been determined by the number in the end product node. Bill sold only one item on Monday, so the probability of him selling items on Monday is 33%, or the total number of items sold divided by the number of items sold by Bill (3/1 x 100 = 33%). Since Tom sold two items on Monday, his Monday sales probability is 66%. Even though Bill sold more furniture than Tom, Tom is still the better salesperson on Mondays.

In the above two scenarios I've tried to provide you with two simple examples that show how classes are naturally organized within the Triadic Continuum. And, while these examples are simple, as I've mentioned before, the process of classification that I've shown stays the same no matter how we increase the number of records. This is one of the powers of the Triadic Continuum.

9

Associations

What is here said of association by resemblance is true of all association. All associa-
tion is by signs. Everything has its subjective or emotional qualities, which are attrib-
uted either absolutely or relatively, or by conventional imputation to anything which
is a sign of it. Charles Peirce[1]

As experience clusters certain ideas into sets, so does the mind too, by its occult nature,
cluster certain ideas into sets. These sets have various forms of connection. The simplest
are sets of things all on one footing and agreeing in each belonging to the set. Such a set
is a class. The clustering of ideas into classes is the simplest form which the association
of ideas by the occult nature of ideas, or of the mind, can take. Charles Peirce[2]

As you will notice by the time you finish reading the four chapters that comprise this part of the book, the word "relationship" is used very broadly in data
mining. Depending on what type of information one is searching for or what
problem one is trying to solve, the relationship may be viewed and defined differently. The first type of complex relationship covered here is called "associations."
Associations in data are broadly defined as interesting correlations of field values
within large data sets. It should be noted in the following quote that the word
"record" corresponds to a path in the structure of a Triadic Continuum.

Associations are items that occur together in a given event or record. Association tools discover rules of the form: If Item A is part of an event, then x percent
of the time (the confidence factor) Item B is part of the event. For example: If
low-fat cottage cheese and non-fat yogurt are purchased, 85 percent of the time
skim milk is purchased as well.[3]

The skim milk example above is an example of one of the most well studied
problems in data mining—called "market basket analysis." As generally defined

Market Basket Analysis is an algorithm that examines a long list of transactions in order to determine which items are most frequently purchased together. It takes its name from the idea of a person in a supermarket throwing all of their items into a shopping cart (a "market basket"). The results can be useful to any company that sells products, whether it's in a store, a catalog, or directly to the customer.[4]

While skim milk and cottage cheese are appropriate examples of market basket analysis, the most often quoted association is that of "beer and diapers." This association, which is often used to explain market basket analysis, hinges on the discovery that beer and diapers are frequently purchased at the same time. Analysts believe that parents with a new child have little else to do on a Saturday night but stay home with the newborn. So, when one of the parents goes out to purchase emergency diapers, he or she pick up a six-pack for themselves.

Market basket analysis is most often used to analyze retail store transactional data to uncover customer-purchasing patterns, where the results of the analysis can be used "to suggest combinations of products for special promotions or sales, devise a more effective store layout, and give insight into brand loyalty and co-branding."[5] However, some have recently applied the rules of market basket analysis to other areas that also contain large banks of information, like that of retail transactions. One such novel application reported in 1999 is using market basket analysis algorithms to detect subject categories of book borrowed from the University of Waikato, in New Zealand. The authors of the report suggest that knowing what books and other resources are being checked out of a library may enable the library sponsors to offer patrons other documents that they may find relevant to their needs, or even as the basis for reorganizing the physical layout of the library to facilitate library usage.

Association Rules

As briefly mentioned above, in data mining the searching for associations is called "association rule mining." In other words, analysts search for the rules that govern how items in data are associated. One association rule that was alluded to above was the association among low-calorie (low-cal) cottage cheese, non-fat yogurt, and skim milk, which can be read in an "if/then" statement: if $x1$ and $x2$, then $x3$. This rule, stated in English, says, if low-cal cottage cheese ($x1$) is purchased and non-fat yogurt ($x2$) is also purchased at the same time, then skim milk is also purchased.

Another characteristic of association rules is that they have confidence values, which just means that there is a percentage associated with the rule. So, restating the example above with a confidence value of 85%, we have:

> If low-cal cottage cheese (x1) is purchased and non-fat yogurt (x2) is also purchased at the same time, then 85 percent of the time skim milk is purchased as well.[6]

Confidence values allow one to predict that a rule is either strong or weak. A high percentage equates to a strong rule, a low percentage, and a weak rule.

Market Basket Analysis Using the Triadic Continuum

The power of the Triadic Continuum in a market basket analysis is in its ability to quickly show associations without having to create or modify complex programs or cubes each time a particle of data is added or deleted. What I mean is that assume in a traditional database world a large supermarket chain stock thousands of items, many of which change names, sizes, or price often. When fields are added, changed, or deleted, the database programmer must make changes to the database design. Those working on database cubes must regenerate or rebuild all or portions of the cube—generally a time intensive task. Ask any database manager and he or she will tell you the cost in time and money is staggering, depending on the amount and frequency of the changes. Often, the entire cube must be rebuilt (a new program must be written) to accommodate changes to the data, or to the queries being asked on the data. So, anything that helps the programmers to quickly find the answers to complex problems, such as market basket analysis, saves them time, which translates into money the company and shareholders are saved.

The following example uses transaction data from a fictitious regional grocery store chain. All of the data is realistic. I've also limited how many transactions are shown so that the resulting Triadic Continuum was not too large to show on one page of this book. However, you need to understand that even adding millions of more transaction records does not slow down how quickly the market basket analysis is done. Because, as you probably understand by now, all of the records don't need to be searched, as in traditional databases, the analysis can be limited to only the specific type of association one needs, in this example market basket analysis.

Before explaining how the Triadic Continuum can quickly analyze market basket associations, I need to set up the scenario for the example.

Assume that Ray D'Antonio, the northeast regional manager for Chuck's Groceries, a chain of 30 supermarkets on the East Coast, has decided after visiting a number of competitors' stores, that his stores appear old fashioned and have little similarity in where and how products are arranged and displayed. Because Chuck's began as a single market that has expanded by buying out failed chain stores, the overall effect is that each store not only looks different, but each store arranges and displays items differently. The regional manager has read up on the topic of brand loyalty, and believes he must do something to make the experience of visiting Chuck's as pleasant and familiar as he can. D'Antonio hires a product placement consultant to help him understand the right methods to arrange and display products so that the visual sales effect is optimized.

The consultant, Maggie Clare, makes a number of standard product placement suggestions, such as displaying children's cereal at the height of children and placing the dairy case on the opposite side of the store from the bakery, causing shoppers to have to walk across the store to buy bread and milk, two items commonly purchased together. By doing this, the customer is given the "opportunity" to purchase items they may not have bought had the bread and milk been positioned next to each other.

While discussing the arrangement of dairy and bakery items, Clare brought up the idea of performing a market basket analysis. After explaining how a market basket analysis might be used, D'Antonio suggests that she speak with the Director of IT, Melissa Williams.

During a meeting between Clare and Williams, the IT Director explains that her department uses traditional databases and that they program database cubes whenever they need to answer big business questions. Williams explains that that approach is time consuming, often taking months to develop new cubes for specific queries. She's afraid that, because her team has never written a cube on which to conduct market basket analysis, that it could take months to accomplish, and she knows that D'Antonio is looking for something more quickly.

Clare suggests a different approach that uses a new technology called the Phaneron, which can be installed, loaded, and ready to query and perform market basket analysis in one-tenth the time as writing a cube from scratch. After jumping a few corporate hurdles, they agree to conduct a pilot market basket analysis on four stores in Maryland.

They know that a record is recorded in their database for every customer transaction, by item and date. With this, other information is kept, such as which store it was sold in, the quantity and the price to name a few. A sample of the pilot data is shown in the database table below.

Store	Store ID	Trans. Date	Trans ID	Man.	Item	Qty.	Price
Highland	1322	05/12/2005	100	Parkay	Butter	1 lb.	$2.34
Highland	1322	05/12/2005	100	Wonder	Bread	16 oz	$1.12
Highland	1322	05/12/2005	100	Bayer	Aspirin	100 tab	$3.52
Reading	555	05/12/2005	255	Children's	Aspirin	500 tab	$5.50
Ellicott	6666	05/16/2005	402	Parkay	Butter	2 lb.	$4.50
Ellicott	6666	05/16/2005	402	Manhattan	Bagels	6	$2.05
Ellicott	6666	05/16/2005	402	Philadelphia	Cheese	1 lb.	$1.25
Greenville	952	05/16/2005	302	Bayer	Aspirin	250 tab	$4.34
Greenville	952	05/16/2005	302	Wonder	Bread	16 oz.	$0.96
Greenville	952	05/16/2005	303	Crest	Toothpaste	6 oz.	$2.56

Figure 9–1

The table above shows only ten records from the thousands of transactions for the time period. As I mentioned above, I've limited the data so that the resulting picture of the Triadic Continuum would fit on a page.

After the IT Director's group loads the pilot transaction data into the Phan-eron software and a Triadic Continuum is created, the resulting structure looks like the following diagram.

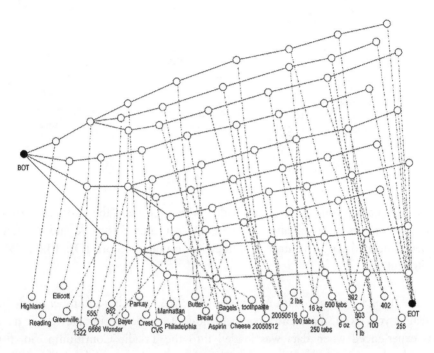

Figure 9–2

Now you can see why I limited it to only ten records, all of which have been loaded into a Triadic Continuum and shown above. While a bit cluttered, it should be obvious by now that for each particle of data that was loaded there is an associated node.

The illustration that follows shows a small section of the main diagram enlarged to show only the eight leftmost nodes.

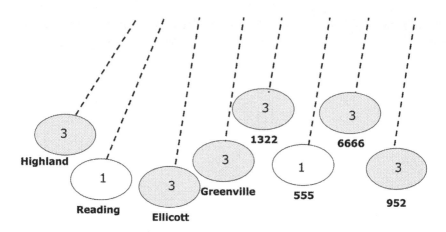

Figure 9–3

In this picture you can see eight nodes, which represent the nodes associated with the four stores: Highland, Reading, Ellicott, and Greenville and the four nodes associated with the store identification numbers (Store ID): 1322, 555, 6666, and 952.

One thing I want to point out is that each of the nodes has a number inside it, which as you recall, represent a count of how often the specific particle of data was experienced when data was loaded into the Triadic Continuum. So, for example, the node for the "Ellicott" store is shown with the number "3" inside to represent the fact that to the moment in time that the diagram represents, the Triadic Continuum had experienced (or loaded in) three records that had the name "Ellicott" associated with them. Similarly, the node representing the node for the "Reading" store is shown with the number "1" inside. Again, to the point in time that this diagram represents, only one record was experienced that had a "Reading" data particle.

As soon as the structure is done being built, it's ready to perform the market basket "association" analytic on. Before explaining how that is done, let me mention something about the previous sentence. In it, I said that "as soon as the structure is done being built," it could be analyzed. I need to mention though that one doesn't need to wait until the structure is completely built before performing analysis or even querying the structure. This is a system that allows you to perform analysis and even ask queries while it is being built—the answers to your questions may change as new data are loaded or the results of the analytics may be different from one minute to the next. This illustrates the real-time nature of the Triadic Continuum. No longer must one wait until all data are loaded to get preliminary answers. Nor, does one have to spend time building a cube, which contains a "snap-shot" of data as it was when the cube began being built—days, even months may have elapsed. No, the Triadic Continuum just keeps getting "smarter" as more data are learned, allowing you to see how the answers to your questions change based on the new input data.

Getting back to the market basket example. Let's assume in our scenario that Clare, the product placement consultant, wants to see what products are purchased in association with other products. She starts with the product "aspirin." Running the Market Basic Analytic, she sets up a simple query that asks, "When aspirin is purchased, what other items are commonly purchased during the same transaction?" A few seconds later she has an answer, butter and eggs.

Here's how the Triadic Continuum came up with that answer based on the pilot data. Take a look at the next illustration that shows the first step.

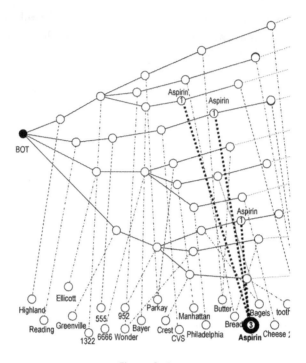

Figure 9–4

The first thing the market basket analytic does is find the variable node for "aspirin," as shown in the diagram above. Since the counter for that node has a count of "3," it immediately knows that there were only three transactions where aspirin was purchased in this sample data set. Then, the analytic traces the asResult path back to all of the nodes associated with it. There are three Result paths, which are shown in the illustration as paths highlighted as darker dotted lines. Next, the analytic traces the path associated with the asCase list leading from each of the nodes associated with aspirin to the node that represents the "market basket identifier," which is the node that is associated with "Transaction ID." This happens because it is looking for every transaction where someone purchased aspirin, and because the "Transaction ID" identifies each basket, only those paths that contain nodes with transactions that are associated with aspirin will be searched. The next diagram shows the result of this last operation.

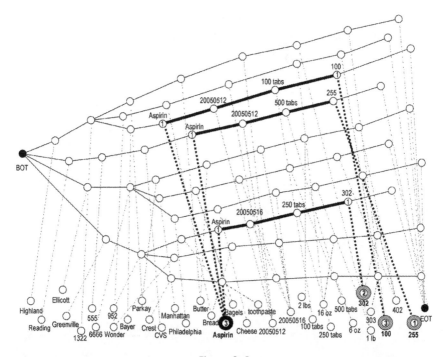

Figure 9–5

Notice in the above diagram that there are there are three Case paths highlighted in thick black lines leading from the nodes representing aspirin forward to
the nodes representing the transaction identifiers associated for each. The Transaction IDs associated with aspirin are the nodes labeled (100), (255), and (302).
Each of these nodes has a highlighted dotted path back along the asResult path to
their associated sensor. For example, "Transaction ID" node (100) is connected
through its asResult path to sensor node (100), which has a count of "3." This
means that two other paths are associated with "Transaction ID" (100), or in
other words that there must be two other items that were purchased in transaction 100 along with aspirin.

"Transaction ID" node (255) is also connected through its asResult path to its
sensor node (255), but this time, its count is only "1," which means that nothing
else was purchased during that transaction but aspirin. Right away the analytic
rules this out of a market basket analysis—nothing else was purchased with aspirin in that transaction. The last "Transaction ID" node (302) has an associated
sensor that contains a count of "2," which means that besides aspirin, there was

one other item in that transaction. The next diagram shows the result of knowing which transaction identifiers are associated with aspirin.

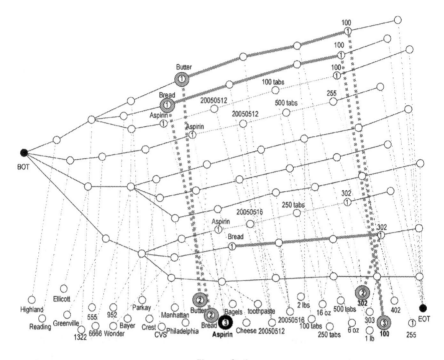

Figure 9–6

To then discover what items were also bought when aspirin was purchased, the analytic simply follows all Result paths connected to sensors (100) and (302). You can see in the diagram that sensor node (100) has two other Result paths (other than the one leading to aspirin). Following those two paths leads to nodes, one in the top record and one in the second most top row, both highlighted in dotted gray lines. From there, the Case path is followed back to the node that represents the item purchased in that transaction. In the case of the top record, if we trace the Case path back, we eventually come to a node that represents Butter. The market basket analytic places this item and its count in an internal calculator until the remaining other paths are searched.

From the Transaction ID (100) node in the second from the top row, high-lighted in solid gray, the Case path is traced back to a node that represents Bread.

The internal calculator places the name of the item into its memory as it does its count.

The Case path from Transaction ID node (302) is traced until the node for the item associated with it is found. In this case it is the node that represents "Bread." Since the item "Bread" is already in the internal calculator, the market basket analytic marks it as and increments the counter to "2" for Bread.

Since the sensor node for Transaction ID 255 had only one transaction, nothing is searched for that ID. Therefore, the market basket analytic is complete. The results indicate that, in this small data set, aspirin is most often purchased with Bread (twice) and Butter (once). As in my other examples, the scope of the example is small, but assume that this is replicated a thousand-fold; the principles and operation is exactly the same, only more paths would be searched, and the speed of today's computers makes that a minor issue. Another key importance, as I mentioned before, is that after the initial data are loaded into the structure, adding more data doesn't mean that the analytic or that the structure need to changed, it simply means that the structure will get larger, but more importantly that the results of the market basket analysis continue to become more accurate.

Market basket analysis is an example of a data relationship that isn't obvious to uncover in large amounts of data, and that's what makes it such a good example of the power of the Triadic Continuum.

10

Patterns in Time

The intellectual life of thought resides in its forms—its patterns. Now there is one pattern which must always be supreme in thought, because it is essentially the pattern of reasoning itself. Charles Peirce[1]

In the last chapter I discussed associations and defined them as events that co-occur in a path. You may have inferred from the discussion that these are events that have already happened, and rightly so. Even though a Triadic Continuum can be built with live transaction data and the associations that are created as data are read can be identified, the associations are still simply historical, albeit nano-second-old historical data.

This chapter deals with anticipated associations—associations that have yet to occur, commonly called patterns or trends. It's possible to predict future events by identifying sequential time-related patterns in the data.

> The mining of sequential patterns is designed to find patterns of discrete events that frequently happen in the same arrangement along a timeline. Like association and clustering, the mining of sequential patterns is among the most popular knowledge discovery techniques that apply statistical measures to extract useful information from large datasets. As our computers become more powerful, we are able to mine bigger datasets and obtain hundreds of thousands of sequential patterns in full detail. With this vast amount of data, we argue that neither data mining nor visualization by itself can manage the information and reflect the knowledge effectively. Subsequently, we apply visualization to augment data mining in a study of sequential patterns in large text corporations.[2]

In the retail environment, "data is mined to anticipate behavior patterns and trends."[3] For example, retailers can make predictions about trends in consumer buying patterns based on the large amounts of data stored in their own transaction databases, in log files on customer use of their Web sites, and even through a mining of their own online or telephone customer service data. You can probably think of many other uses in banking, sales, and stock market transactions where knowing the likelihood that certain events may occur is an advantage.

But, there are also many other areas in which prediction is useful, besides predicting the next lotto winning number that is. In law enforcement an entire field is developing called "crime mapping" that uses crime data of past crimes to spot crime trends and forecast potential targets and hot spots.[4]

Single Variable Prediction

As a quick aside, Single Variable Prediction was the first analytic that Mazzagatti created after she discovered the Triadic Continuum. From her reading of Peirce and of others in cognitive science, she believes that single variable prediction is the mechanism that the brain uses to make predictions as to what will happen every second of our conscious lives. Single variable prediction is extremely simple, but simple in an elegant way. Without complexity, it predicts the likelihood, or probability, of a given single event (single variable) happening based on known factors. It can be calculated alone or in multiple contexts (by setting constraints on the data set). In other words, you can predict the likelihood of one single event occurring, or you can make predictions that are more specific by limiting the records for Bill to only those that include one or more other variables. For example, as explained earlier, assume that you want to know the number of transactions associated with the salesman Bill. In this example, "Bill" is the single variable on which the prediction will occur. But, if you want to know how many sofas Bill sells, "sofas" and "sold" help to "constrain" the data to only those values within the records associated with the salesman "Bill."

In the following example, I use historical and real-time crime data from a fictional city police department. As I've done before, the data is realistic, but I've limited how many events (crimes) to show.

In our scenario, a recent rash of muggings has occurred and crime "forecasters" want to know the likelihood of muggings occurring on one historically bad street corner: 5th Street and Evans Ave., simply labeled "5th St." on the diagrams that follow.

Whenever a crime is reported, either through a 911 call, a telephone call to a police station, or by an officer at a crime scene entering the information directly into a patrol car computer, the data are fed into the main crime database. Within this database there may be thousands of records dealing with crimes that have either been committed or attempted.

In the following example, there are 90 records, which have been entered over a six-month period. For simplicity, each record contains only five fields: category of crime, location, time of day, whether the crime was attempted or committed, and whether the location of the crime was poorly lit or well lit. Three sample records might look like the following:

Category	Location	Time	Disposition	Lighting
Mugging	5th and Evans	Night	Committed	Poor
Mugging	B Avenue and L	Night	Attempted	Well
Robbery	B Avenue and L	Night	Committed	Well

Figure 10–1

The data are then read into a Triadic Continuum from which a crime forecaster can perform predictions upon it. The following diagram represents 90 records of the resulting Triadic Continuum.

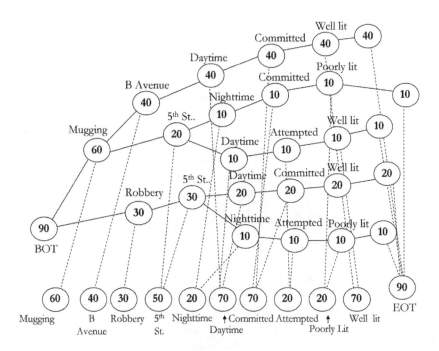

Figure 10–2

Next, the forecaster defines the variable on which to run the Single Variable Prediction analytic. In our example the variable is set to "mugging." At this point the forecaster could run the analytic, but decides to further limit the category "muggings" to those that were actually committed and committed at the corner of 5th and Evans. After identifying the constraints, the forecaster runs the analytic on the crime data already in the Triadic Continuum.

While running, the first thing the Single Variable Prediction analytic does is to constrain the data by "Location" (5th and Evans). It does this by tracing the asResult paths from the "5th St." sensor back to all nodes associated with 5th St. and Evans as shown in the diagram below highlighted with a thick black dotted line.

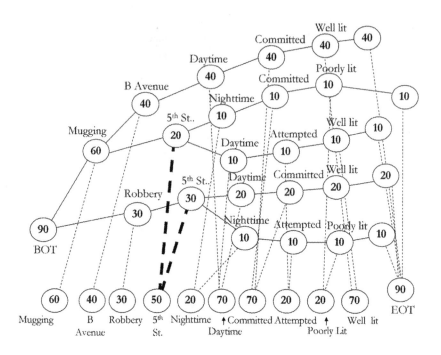

Figure 10–3

Next the analytic traces the Case path leading from these nodes forward toward the EOT node for that path. When a node associated with the next constraint, the disposition "Committed" is found along the path, the analytic continues to the end of the path. If it does not find a node associated with "committed" along the path, the path is discounted, but if "committed" is a part of that path, the EOT node and the number in its counter is held in memory. In the picture below, two EOT nodes have been found that terminate a path that contains nodes associated with both "5th St." and "Committed." One has a counter that registers "10" and the other registers "20." These numbers represent the number of crimes that contain both of the constraints.

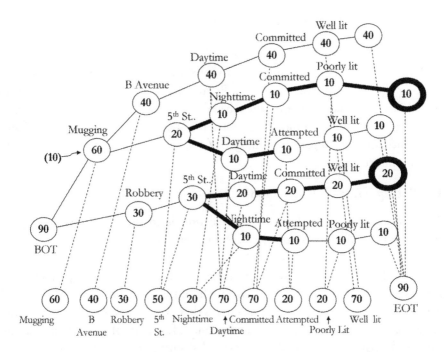

Figure 10–4

The analytic then takes the number in the counter of the two EOT nodes and adds them together for a total of 30. This is the sum of all crimes "committed" at "5th and Evans."

The next thing the analytic does is starting at these two EOT nodes, it traces backward along the asCase path searching for the main focus of the operation, the crime of mugging. Notice on the proceeding diagram that only one of the two paths terminates at a node that is associated with mugging (node 10). The analytic takes the number from the counter in the EOT node associated with that path, which in the example is "10," and divides the number already stored "30" into "10" for a probability of 33%. Or to answer the forecaster's original question, there is a 33% likelihood of a "mugging" being committed on the corner of 5th Street and Evans Ave.

And finally, with that knowledge, it is the job of those responsible to decide, based on the forecast, to either act upon the prediction by adding more police, better lights, or television cameras or to try and determine the root cause of the problem.

And while finding the right action to solve the problem is often difficult, calculating the actual prediction is not. Prediction is based on the likelihood, or probability of something occurring, based on known factors. In other words, there's no need to pre-define or set probabilities as is done in other types of analytics and data structures; they fall out of the actual data that is in the Triadic Continuum structure.

Predicting Time-Related Events

Another way to use single variable prediction is to predict events as they are related to time. As an example, let's assume that the owner of the furniture store where Bill and Tom are employed knows from experience that January and February are slow sales months in the furniture business. She wants to predict which items she should discount and which she should not—items that commonly sell well should be priced as normal while items that don't sell well can be heavily discounted. Using single variable prediction and a few years of transaction data she can see the patterns in time that exist in sales during the months of January and February. Then using this information, she can decide which items to discount. With this information she may decide to increase inventory on items that show a trend toward selling out.

Here is how she would do this. Using historical data from as many years as she has—the more years the better since the trends will be more pronounced and accurate the larger the data set. Next she would load all of the data into a Triadic Continuum. The resulting continuum might look something like the following.

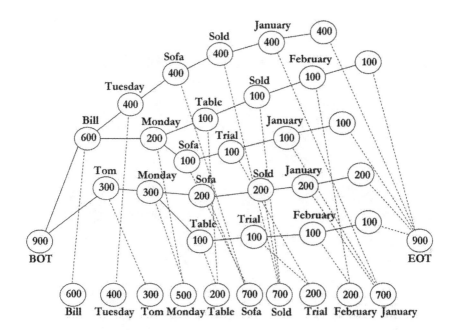

Figure 10–5

Next, the owner identifies the variables on which to run the Single Variable Prediction analytic. In this example she picks the variable items "Sold," and further constrains the data to only those sold in "January" and only those sold in February. She then runs the analytic on the furniture store transactional data already in the Triadic Continuum.

The first thing the Single Variable Prediction analytic does is to constrain the data by items "Sold." It does this by tracing the asResult paths from the "Sold" elemental node back to all nodes associated with "Sold" as shown in the diagram below highlighted by three black dotted lines.

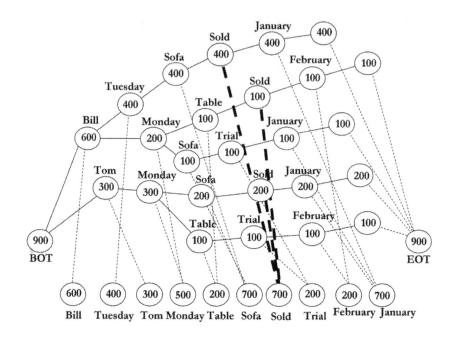

Figure 10–6

Next the analytic traces the Case path leading from these "Sold" nodes forward toward the EOT node for that path. Because she identified "January" first, the analytic first tries to determine the number of items "Sold" in "January." It does this in the same fashion explained earlier. When a node associated with "January" is found along the path, the analytic continues to the end of the path. If it does not find a node associated with "January" along the path, the path is discounted, but if "January" is a part of that path, the EOT node and the number in its counter is held in memory. In the picture below, two EOT nodes have been found that end a path that contains nodes associated with both "Sold" and "January." One has a counter that registers 400 and the other registers 200, or in other words, these numbers represent the number of transactions that contain both of the constraints, "Sold" and "January," or a total of 600 items sold in January. This information is temporarily stored until the Single Variable Prediction runs using the variables "Sold" and this time, "February," because it was identified before "January."

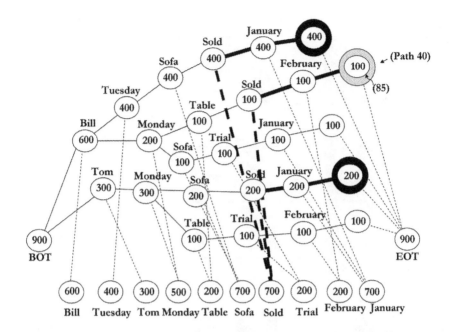

Figure 10–7

The same process occurs as was just explained, but this time the analytic uncovers only one path from a "Sold" node that continues to a node for February. The end product node (node 85) for that path (path 40) contains a counter that registers 100, or 100 items sold in February.

To finish this example, assume that the Single Variable Prediction analytic contains a graphing feature that takes information and represents it visually. The following figure is a bar graph showing the patterns over time, or in other words the trend in sales, specifically in the months of January and February, for this fictional furniture store.

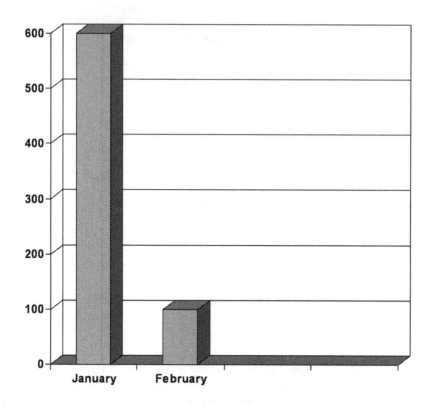

Figure 10–8

Using the knowledge she's gained from doing this, the owner of the furniture store can make informed promotional and marketing decisions based on an analysis of patterns (trends) that occur over time.

Before ending this chapter, I want to mention again that many of the examples I choose to use in this book are purposely simple to illustrate and educate you to how information is realized in the Triadic Continuum. That said; don't let the simplicity of the above example fool you—performing trend analysis on large amounts of data using the structure of the Triadic Continuum is much more efficient and quick than conventional data structures.

11

K Clusters

The clustering of ideas into classes is the simplest form which the association of ideas by the occult nature of ideas, or of the mind, can take. Charles Peirce[1]

Clusters are data items that "are grouped according to logical relationships."[2] By "logical relationships" I mean that there is some inherent grouping of specific items in the data. Unlike classification that organizes data into categories based on their attributes and characteristics, clustering sorts items into groups by the magnitude of their relations to one another. The goal of clustering is to find groups that differ from one another, as well as to find similarities among members of the group.[3]

Analyzing data to find clusters has practical application in widely diverse disciplines such as genetics, business, and organizational development. In biology, clustering is used, among other methods, to arrange genes according to similarity in the pattern of how the genes are outwardly expressed. The output of this clustering enables biologists to graphically visualize relationships among data, which presents the data "in a form intuitive for biologists."[4]

Cluster analysis has been found valuable in business settings, such as market analysis, where clusters can be found to identify market segments or consumer affinities. A simple example is in the marketing of credit card offers to specific demographics. For example, assume a large bank is offering a credit card to its customers. The marketing staff wants to determine who best to market the initial offer to through a series of telephone calls or letters. The staff feels that it would like to target approximately 25% of its current customer base, but wonders which 25% would be best to target. Using cluster analysis they can select specific variable criteria to analyze. For example, assume they select income level and home ownership as their two variables. Running this analysis on their data they determine that approximately 25% of their customers cluster around two variables: an income of over $100,000 per year and owning their own home. Another way to look at it is that from the analysis of their historical customer data they discover that there is a cluster of approximately 25% that meets two key variables, home ownership and a specific level of income. So, through the use of cluster analysis, the marketers decide to send letters to only those families and individuals who meet these criteria.

Another example of a business application is in the regulation of business economics where clustering has been used to analyze the transfer prices at which property is exchanged between firms. How prices are set has "important implications for the cross border allocation of multinational income."[5] Using clustering techniques allow regulators to identify comparable transactions from within pricing data to assess the effectiveness of policies and regulations.

The social sciences have also found that clustering techniques can help in the understanding of how businesses and organizations accomplish work and share knowledge. Most businesses and large organizations have data captured within different databases. Often a single company will have separate databases that contain general employee demographic data, payroll, organizational, and other types of disparate data. There is also data kept in other computer networks within a company such as emails, Internet usage patterns, corporate directories, and organizational charts, to name but a few. Data spread throughout all of these databases is being used to find the social relationships among people within companies. Those who study social networks broadly define "social relationships" as "the mapping and measuring of networks and flows between people, groups, organizations, animals, computers, or other information and knowledge processing entities."[6] Business and management consultants use the methods of discovering networks in companies to identify the relationships and links between the organization as it appears on paper in organizational charts and how the organization functions in practice—and it's generally not the same. With most companies, organizational charts list how work is accomplished, theoretically in the hierarchical organization, while in practice, work is more often done not in an orderly hierarchy, but in more chaotic linkages of people-to-people relations.

Social Networks

It's with this idea of clusters in mind that I will discuss a discipline called Social Network Analysis, which developed to search out "causes and consequences of relations between people and among sets of people rather than on the features of individuals."[7] An example of social networks that most everyone knows is that of the game "Six Degrees of Separation," also known as the "Six Degrees of Kevin Bacon." This game, which was made popular in the 1990s through the Internet, says that everyone is connected to everyone else by six connections or less. Players try to connect a specific individual to the actor Kevin Bacon in six or less connections. The theoretical basis behind the six degrees of separation came from a series of experiments in the mid 1960s by Harvard sociologist Stanley Milgram, and what he later called the "Small World Hypothesis."

Less familiar to most of us is the research being done by social scientists and management theorists on how human relationships affect how work gets accomplished and knowledge gets moved and shared in large corporations and organizations. In this context, those who study and analyze social networks use statistical tools and analysis techniques to uncover the hidden clusters of relations that exist in a company that no one ever really sees or understands. The web and flow of work, communication (or lack thereof), power, corporate politics, status, and a multitude of other factors all come together to form known and unknown relationships in a company or organization. Often these statistical and analytic tools and techniques discover some of the hidden relationships that exist, but more often than not, fail to find the more complex and subtle ones. Plus, the methods used to gather the data and information about the social network often comes from person-to-person interviews and questionnaires—all of which are imprecise for a number of reasons, the least of which is writing or saying anything that may have an impact on an employee's own success in the company or organization. No matter how trusting employees are of the confidentiality of the interview or questionnaire, they may feel uncomfortable being candid and may feel the need to couch their comments. So, analysts receive imprecise and often wrong information about the nature of the organization. However, some technologies are beginning to use the tacit information found in memos, emails, and phone logs that may tell the true story of who works with whom and how the social network of a company or organization really works. To show an example of how social networks are discovered, I'm going to use a scenario developed by the Network Roundtable at the University of Virginia.

The Network Roundtable, a consortium of academic and business organizations who sponsor research on network and management issues, believe in the importance of understanding the social relationships and network of a company and explain that this knowledge can help improve strategic decision-making, promote innovation, and develop communities of practice. One of their fundamental principles is that "many strategically important networks do not reside on the formal organization chart."[8]

The following example scenario uses the organizational structure of a fictitious petroleum company as it is viewed in its organizational chart.[9] As you can see, the organizational chart below shows that senior vice president Mr. Jones leads the Exploration and Production division. As you can also see, Jones has three people who report directly to him: Mr. Williams, Ms. Taylor, and Ms. Campbell, each of whom manage the Exploration, Drilling, and Production teams respectively.

Exploration and Production

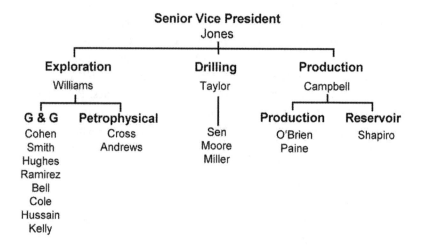

Figure 11–1

Looking at the chart, one may assume that Mr. Jones, since he's the Vice President of the entire division interacts with his direct reports equally in any given period of time, say in a given month. However, in the real world, some managers may need less supervision and direction than others, while some VPs are more hands on than others, and every combination in between. In our scenario, the President of the company, Mr. Holloway, notices problems in the operation and Exploration and Production division and after unsuccessfully trying to solve them, hires an organization and management consultant to help locate the cause or causes.

An organizational consultant with knowledge of social networks would know that the needed data about the relationships in the company come, not only from sources like the organizational chart, but also from employee interviews and questionnaires. They also know that there are software tools available to help them analyze and graphically visualize the information, turning data into digital maps that chart relationships and linkages.

As it stands today, organizational consultants would use the techniques and tools available and be able to locate some interesting relationships and knowledge about the company. They would probably have their most success in locating knowledge that is open to all, or explicit knowledge as it's known. Explicit knowledge is generally available in text, tables, diagrams, and other written or archived sources. Explicit knowledge is fairly easy to obtain, but not always accurate. For example the information found in an organizational chart may show the organizational picture of how the company is structured, but not how it's really organized and run. But, there's more to it than what explicit information and knowledge show; there's also knowledge and relations that are not, or cannot, be articulated. These relationships and knowledge are called "tacit," coined by Michael Polanyi, who explains tacit knowledge by saying, "We know more than we can tell."[10] It's assumed that many of us have knowledge of situations and relations that we consciously don't want to tell others, but we also have things we cannot verbally articulate, aren't willing to articulate, or, in the most extreme case, we have knowledge that we ourselves don't know we have—it's invisible to us, either through psychological repression or through the aging process.

However, using the Triadic Continuum, someone like a management or organizational consultant may simply begin by requesting a listing of those corporate database records that contain emails and a log of phone calls for all of those in the Exploration and Production division. Used in place of, or with data from interviews and questionnaires, the consultant can input data into the Triadic Continuum, which as I've stated numerous times, finds the relationships in the chaotic clutter of the data.

In the following scenario, assume that the consultant has asked for all of the emails that the members of the Exploration and Production division have sent to one another over the past few months. The following table shows a small listing of the communication between members of the Exploration and Production division over a given period of time. This structured data could easily be gathered by scanning and logging the names in the "To" field and the "From" field in achieved email messages.

Employee	Communicates with
Jones	Williams, Cole
Williams	Jones, Andrews, Taylor
Taylor	Bell, Cole, Miller, Williams, Sen
Campbell	O'Brian, Shapiro, Paine
Cohen	Cole, Kelly, Cross
Smith	Kelly
Hughes	Kelly, Cole, Ramirez
Ramirez	Hughes, Hussain, Sen
Bell	Ramirez, Cole, Taylor
Cole	Cohen, Kelly, Hughes, Bell, Taylor, Miller, Andrews, Jones
Hussain	Cross, Ramirez
Kelly	Cohen, Smith, Hughes, Cole
Cross	Cohen, Hussain, Moore
Andrews	Cole, Williams
Sen	Taylor
Moore	Cross
Miller	Cole, Taylor
O'Brian	Shapiro, Campbell
Paine	Cole, Shapiro, Campbell
Shapiro	O'Brian, Campbell, Paine, Cole

Figure 11–2

The next table shows who reports to whom and is exerted from the corporate directory. This should be the same as the information found in the organization chart.

Employee	Reports to
Jones	
Williams	Jones
Taylor	Jones
Campbell	Jones
Cohen	Williams
Smith	Williams
Hughes	Williams
Ramirez	Williams
Bell	Williams
Cole	Williams
Hussain	Williams
Kelly	Williams
Cross	Williams
Andrews	Williams
Sen	Taylor
Moore	Taylor
Miller	Taylor
O'Brian	Campbell
Paine	Campbell
Shapiro	Campbell

Figure 11–3

Let's assume that the management consultant has decided to use the Triadic Continuum to identify the social network of the Exploration and Production division. Since the information that the consultant has is from separate data sets:

emails and organizational chart information, he loads both of these disparate data sets into the Triadic Continuum. Once loaded, a triadic structure is built from the incoming data. This data forms an interlocking tree that looks like Figure 11–4. Notice in the diagram that I have purposely made the asResult (dotted) lines a lighter gray in order to make the rest of the diagram more readable. I've also made the asCase (solid) lines thicker and darker for data from the organization chart data set and left the asCase lines for data from the email data set a regular solid line.

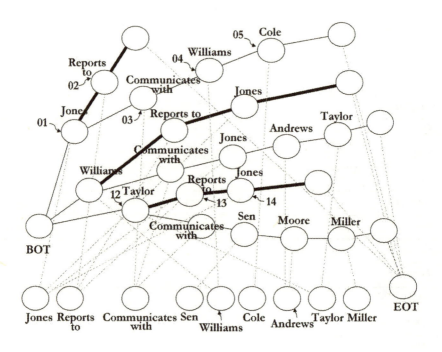

Figure 11–4

The diagram above illustrates some of the less than obvious relations that exist within the data. The Triadic Continuum represented in the diagram contains only those records that deal with the communications between and among the four managers of the division: Jones, Williams, Taylor, and Campbell. A management consultant may have included all of the others in the division, but I purposely left them out to make it easier to see one of the main relationships that exist, and can be seen by looking at the data as represented in a Triadic Continuum. Notice in the diagram that I've numbered many of the nodes within the structure to make it easier to refer to and explain.

One of the most interesting social relationships shown in the data is one surrounding Mr. Jones, the Vice President of the division. You can see in the above diagram that after the communication and org chart information has been loaded into the structure, the resulting Triadic Continuum has records for the data representing who Mr. Jones communicates with and reports to. This is shown beginning at node 01, which represents Mr. Jones and node number 02 that represents the field "Reports to" in the figure above. While I've already mentioned in the above introduction to this scenario that Mr. Jones reports to Mr. Holloway, notice that Holloway isn't represented anywhere in the diagram. If you look at the information that was loaded into the Triadic Continuum, as shown in Figures 11–2 and 11–3, you'll notice that Holloway isn't listed in either of them. Even though he's the President of the company, the data that the management consultant used to build the Triadic Continuum did not include his name or information about him. Other data sources with information about Holloway most likely do exist in company databases, but the Triadic Continuum that was built in this specific example does not contain any. You might think that the fact that we did not find anything about Holloway is insignificant, but it illustrates a fundamental principle of data structures: if the data isn't in the structure, it doesn't matter how powerful the structure is, the information is still not there. However, the Triadic Continuum allows you to easily identify information and relationships that do not exist in the data, which is often as important as finding information and relationships that are in the data.

Next, let's look at the record that begins with node 01 and traverses through node 03 and on through nodes 04 and 05. This pathway represents the first record from the "Communication" data found in Figure 11–2. What this shows is that during the period of time represented by the emails and phone logs, Mr. Jones communicated with only two people: Cole and Williams. We know that from the org chart that Jones has three direct reports, Williams, Taylor, and Campbell, but from what we see through the Triadic Continuum, he's only communicated with one of those people who actually reports to him: Mr. Williams. Hopefully he communicates with his other direct reports, Taylor and Campbell, in person.

Now, let's look at both of Jones's direct reports in more detail. If we first look at the nodes representing Ms. Taylor, we can see that while she reports to Jones (nodes 12, 13, and 14), she communicates with Sen, Moore, and Miller, all direct reports of hers. Not bad, at least she communicates with the people who report to her. However, there's no communication initiated by her and directed to Mr. Jones. So, we see that neither of them initiates any type of communication. If we look at the nodes for Ms. Campbell we see a similar situation. Campbell communicates with her direct reports, but never with her manager, Mr. Jones.

While the relationships shown in these pathways are not conclusive of any major problem, they may bear watching.

"Antisocial" Networks

Another possible application of understanding social network relationships is in the area of terrorism. It doesn't take an expert to realize that after 9/11 there is a need to find tools to uncover hidden "social" networks—terrorists communicate with one another, as do members of other organizations. And, when it comes to global security issues, it's extremely important to determine who is talking to whom in a terrorist organization.

The following example uses a hypothetical database in an organization like the U. S. Department of Homeland Security, which we can safely assume is filled with records of telephone calls made throughout the world. These telephone records consist of telephone numbers and the telephone number called from that extension. In a traditional database, there might be records that look like those in the table below.

This telephone number	Called this telephone number
610-555-7123	415-555-8760
610-555-7123	212-555-9905

Figure 11–5

Each day in the US there are millions of telephone calls placed from millions of phones. A database holding only the data shown above for all of those millions of calls would be huge, larger than most used today. To find out who the caller with the phone number 610-555-7123 called would be pretty simple. All you have to do is ask the computer to look up all the records that have that target number in it. It might take some time because the way a computer database works is that it will search thorough every record looking for that specific number. The key thing to understand is that it looks through **all** of the records. With a database that contains millions, maybe billions of telephone call records, this process might take days to accomplish. If you wanted to find not only who the target number called, but who the people that he called also called, the process gets more complex, and it takes a lot longer. What you're asking the traditional database to do is locate the social network for the target number.

If you used the Triadic Continuum instead of a traditional database to hold the telephone data, finding the social network relations hidden in the data becomes a much quicker and much simpler process. Let me explain why.

As I've explained earlier, the power of the Triadic Continuum is that it holds the relationships between and among data in its data structure. The software that searches through the Triadic Continuum doesn't need to look through the entire data; it only looks for the one instance of the target number and then searches only those paths associated with that number not through every record. To see this more clearly, look at the following picture of the social network of a suspected terrorist, who is represented by the letter "a."

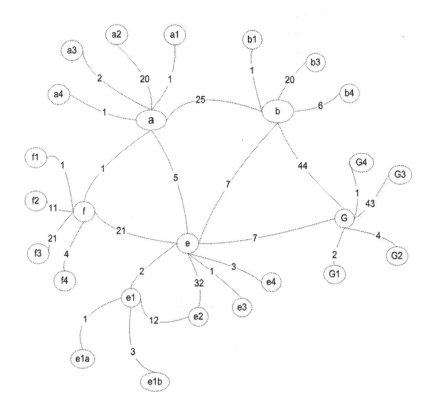

Figure 11–6

Assume in the figure that each circle with a letter represents a person with a different telephone number. For example, the circle with the letter "a" may represent a suspected terrorist whose telephone number 610-555-7123. This person had made phone calls to seven other telephone numbers, which is shown by the lines connecting the circles. In Figure 11–6, "a" has made 25 calls to "b," one call each to "a1," "a4," and "f," 20 calls to "a2," two calls to "a2," and five calls to "e." Assume now that the Department of Homeland Security checks all of the numbers called by "a" and finds that "a1" is the local pizza restaurant and "a4" is another innocuous number. The remaining numbers, especially those made to person "e" and person "f" are further investigated because, as it turns out, they are international numbers.

Using the ability of the Triadic Continuum to discover clusters within a social network, the investigators can easily see the relationships that exist within all of this disparate data. No longer are large amounts of data overwhelming.

In the last few chapters I've tried to show how it is possible to input particles of data that already have a known relationship, such as data coming into the structure via a traditional database, or to input disparate, seemingly unrelated bits of data, like those in the terrorist example, and build a Triadic Continuum that contains associations, classes, and relationships that previously have been difficult or impossible to discover. The Triadic Continuum, as Mazzagatti has said is a model of what is really being experienced, as data are input. In traditional data-bases, the model that is created is a representation of what the person who puts it together thinks it should be, not what it really is.

I've also tried to show that how, once data are in the structure that it becomes knowledge that can be "realized," not simply searched for and sometimes "found" like in databases.

In the next chapter I'll talk about some of the other characteristics and strengths of the Triadic Continuum, both as it relates to computer data struc-tures, and its implications to other sciences as well.

12

Experiential Probability

Probability, they say, measures the state of our knowledge, and ignorance is denoted by the probability 1/2. But I apprehend that the expression "the probability of an event" is an incomplete one. A probability is a fraction whose numerator is the frequency of a specific kind of event, while its denominator is the frequency of a genus embracing that species. Charles Peirce[1]

... all knowledge is based on experience ... Charles Peirce[2]

One of the simplest definitions of probability that I could find, defined it as "The likelihood that a given event will occur: *little probability of rain tonight.*"[3] The word "chance" is also a synonym for probability. This is often used when we ask what the chance of a particular event occurring is—we're asking what the probability (or likelihood) that the particular event will occur.

Those of us who are not mathematicians are most comfortable discussing probability and chance in terms of betting or wagering. Texas Hold'em poker has recently become quite popular in the U.S. with online poker sites and live games springing up everywhere. In Texas Hold'em each player is dealt two cards face down. These first two cards are known as the hole or pocket cards. Students of the game know that the probability (or chance) of being dealt two aces, called "pocket aces," from a deck of 52 cards is 221 to 1 (221/1). That is, you have one chance in 221 that you will be dealt two aces. This is derived from the fact that "there are 52 ways to pick the first card and 51 ways to pick the second card and two ways to order the two cards yielding $52 \times 51 \div 2 = 1,326$ possible outcomes of being dealt two cards (also ignoring order). This gives a probability of being

dealt two aces of $\dfrac{6}{1326} = \dfrac{1}{221}$ [4]

In gaming, probability is generally expressed as a chance, like 220 to 1. However, probability is generally expressed elsewhere in terms of a percentage. So, the probability of being dealt pocket aces is 0.45%. Or,

$$\frac{X}{100} = \frac{1}{221}$$

$$X = (1/221) * 100$$

$$X = 0.45\%$$

But probability isn't only about gambling. "We use probability all the time; from pool to physics, and from craps to car insurance. The laws of probability are well known and fairly simple, and they even appear to work. What we *don't* know as a species is what a probability actually means."[5]

Naïve Probability

In the example above, I used playing cards purposely to illustrate what Mazzagatti calls "naive probability," or probability "lacking in worldly experience." When mathematicians or gamblers list the probability of your being dealt pocket aces, they already know the entire set of possibilities within which probability can be determined; it gains no benefit from experience. In a deck of playing cards the entire set of possibilities is 52—the 52 cards in a regulation deck. Said in mathematical parlance, the set of possibilities is limited to 52—after dealing the first card, that card can no longer be dealt; it's possible that any other card in the deck could be dealt, but not the one already dealt.

Whenever the *set of possibilities* is known, naive probability is the method used to determine the chance of a specific occurrence, for example the chance of being dealt pocket aces.

Another example of naive probability is one that has baffled some students for years, the probability of the coin toss. When teaching introductory probability in math classes, instructors from elementary school to graduate level often use the example of flipping a two-headed coin. So the scenario goes that each time you flip a two-headed coin, the probability of the coin landing heads up is 50% and landing tails up is 50%. As any good math teacher will teach, before the first flip the odds are 50/50 that a heads or a tails will land up. That same teacher will tell you that after 99 flips the chance of the one hundredth flip landing heads up (or tails up) is still 50/50. Expressed in terms of naive probability, the set of possibilities of a two-headed coin is two—on one side of the coin is the heads and on the other side is the tails.

Mazzagatti will tell you that besides this traditional interpretation of probability, like that expressed in the examples of pocket aces and flipping coins, there is another, which she believes is how Peirce interpreted probability. Different than the mathematicians' traditional naïve probability, we call this other perception "experiential" probability.

Experiential Probability

The key to understanding experiential probability is that it is based on experience or on an infinite set of possibilities. As I mentioned above, using coin flipping to explain probability baffles some students. I know this from experience. In a past career I was a biology teacher and taught simple probability within the context of genetics. I can remember students who would challenge my assertion that the probability of a coin turning up heads was still 50% after the last five flips had all turned up heads. As I think back on it now, each year one or two truly inquisitive students would push back at this interpretation of probability, when he or she would intuit that it seemed more likely that the probability was higher for a coin turning up tails after seeing five heads turn up in a row. Having only my knowledge of traditional (naive) probability, and my power as the teacher, I could only laugh and explain that a coin only has two sides and so the probability was 50/50.

So, in terms of naïve probability, each flip of a two-headed coin produces a probability of 50/50, but what if we shift the focus of this and think of this in terms of the experience of the person flipping the coin?

To explain experiential probability, Mazzagatti uses a story about a child and a black dog. In the story a young child, upon her first encounter with a dog of any kind is bitten by the dog, which just happens to have a black coat. Let's say that some time goes by where in she doesn't see another dog. When she next encounters a different black dog, we might say that the probability of her being bitten by the dog are 50/50, for in terms of being bitten by a dog, the set of possibilities (in naïve probability) is two—being bitten or not bitten. But, in terms of experiential probability, the child's experience tells her that all black dogs bite, since in her experience she has seen only one black dog, which has bitten her. Said another way, her experience tells her that 100% of black dogs bite. It's only after being around this second gentle dog, and not being bitten that her experiential probability becomes 50/50. To take it a step further, upon her next positive encounter with a black dog, her experiential probability of being bitten becomes 33.3% (once bitten, twice not).

Again, I know that this example may seem simplistic, but there are others who believe that traditional naive probability isn't the only type of probability or that probability may work differently than we have been led to believe. For example, mathematicians have known for years that certain numbers appear more often than others. In 1881, Simon Newcomb, an astronomer and someone who also played a role in Charles Peirce's life, made an interesting observation while using logarithm tables. He noticed that the pages that were the most worn were those where the logarithms began with the number one. And, those beginning with the number two were more used and dirtier than those that began with three and so on, where those beginning with the number nine seemed to be the least used. In theory, this shouldn't be. Or, in terms of naive probability this shouldn't be. The set of possibilities of numbers is 10 (0–9). Since the log tables don't start with the number zero, there are nine possible numbers that can begin a logarithm (1–9), or a possibility set of nine. If this is true and naive probability is the rule, each of the nine numbers from 1–9 have an equal probability of being used. Newcomb published a paper on his findings in the *American Journal of Mathematics*, [6] but got little notice until 1938 when Dr. Frank Benford, a physicist working for the General Electric Company rediscovered and popularized it.

> A crude and approximate statement of Benford's law, also called the first-digit law, is that in lists of numbers from many real-life sources of data, the leading digit is 1 almost one-third of the time, and further, larger numbers occur as the leading digit with less and less frequency as they grow in magnitude, to the point that 9 is the leading digit less than one time in twenty.

> This counter-intuitive result applies to a wide variety of figures from the natural world or of social significance—including electricity bills, street addresses, stock prices, population numbers, death rates, lengths of rivers, physical and mathematical constants, and processes described by power laws (which are very common in nature).[7]

It appears that probability isn't as simple as we've always been taught to believe, that it might be interpreted in different ways and that other laws may govern aspects of it that can't be seen at first glance. So, is probability different than we've always thought of it? Some would say, including I believe Peirce and definitely Mazzagatti, that probability is more than simple naive probability, that experiential probability does exist and functions within our thought or knowledge processes.

During his lifetime, Peirce wrote extensively on topics in mathematics and logic. Mazzagatti believes that Peirce was constantly searching for foundational explanations and examples that would help illustrate his theory of signs as the way to view all human understanding and cognition. You get a sense of this when he wrote, "Begin, if you will, by calling logic the theory of the conditions which determine reasonings to be secure."[8] And, he uses probability to bolster his ideas. In the following passage Peirce is explaining that there is a type of probability that is experiential and that the probability of an event occurring can be determined experientially, as it occurs.

> There are those to whom the idea of an unknown probability seems an absurdity. Probability, they say, measures the state of our knowledge, and ignorance is denoted by the probability 1/2. But I apprehend that the expression "the probability of an event" is an incomplete one. A probability is a fraction whose numerator is the frequency of a specific kind of event, while its denominator is the frequency of a genus embracing that species. Now the expression in question names the numerator of the fraction, but omits to name the denominator. There is a sense in which it is true that the probability of a perfectly unknown event is one half; namely, the assertion of its occurrence is the answer to a possible question answerable by "yes" or "no," and of all such questions just half the possible answers are true. But if attention be paid to the denominators of the fractions, it will be found that this value of 1/2 is one of which no possible use can be made in the calculation of probabilities.[9]

There's a lot of good information packed into the quote above. Let's take it apart and see what he is saying in terms of how I've defined naive and experiential probability.

In the first two sentences, Peirce is saying that there are those who believe only in naive probability, where the outcome of every event has "the probability ½." Those who believe this would think it absurd to believe in an experiential (unknown until the experience) probability.

Let's skip the next few sentences for a minute and pick up with the sentence, "There is a sense in which it is true that the probability of a perfectly unknown event is one half; namely, the assertion of its occurrence is the answer to a possible question answerable by "yes" or "no," and of all such questions just half the possible answers are true."[10] Here Peirce is saying that when the set of possibilities is known, say for example "yes" or "no," that there is such a thing as naive probability. But, then he goes on to say in the last sentence that "... if attention be paid to the denominators of the fractions, it will be found that this value of 1/ 2 is one of which no possible use can be made in the calculation of probabilities."[11]

At this point you may be wondering why an understanding of the nominator and denominator seems to be so important to Peirce and his understanding of experiential probability. That's what Mazzagatti thought as well until she understood the far-reaching implications and applications of the Triadic Continuum, and this only became apparent as she began to work with the Bill and Tom scenario.

As you may remember from an earlier chapter, the Bill and Tom scenario was one of the first things Mazzagatti used to explain the Triadic Continuum. The Bill and Tom scenario consists of nine records for a fictitious furniture store in Pennsylvania and New Jersey. The following diagram was used earlier to show these nine records in a Triadic Continuum.

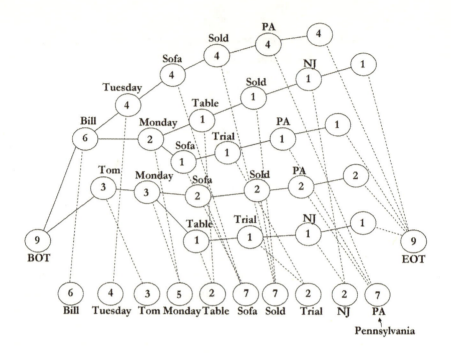

Figure 12–1

Let's assume that the query we want to pose in the Bill and Tom Triadic Continuum is, "What is the probability that a transaction (a sale or a trial) will occur in Pennsylvania?" This is where the first part of the quote above, where Peirce says, "A probability is a fraction whose numerator is the frequency of a specific kind of event …" comes in. In the Bill and Tom nine-record scenario, the "specific kind of event" is the number of transactions occurring in Pennsylvania. To find this we simply search the Triadic Continuum for the elemental node associated with "Pennsylvania," which in the figure above is seven. The number "7" is therefore the numerator, or the frequency of a specific kind of event.

The second phrase in the above Peirce quote reads, "… while its denominator is the frequency of a genus embracing that species." In other words, if the species is the seven Pennsylvania records, the genus is the total number of records in the Triadic Continuum, or nine.

To determine the probability that a transaction will occur in Pennsylvania, one has only to divide the numerator (7) by the denominator (9), which even a theoretical mathematician will tell you is often 77%.

But what happens five minutes, an hour, or two weeks later when the data in the Triadic Continuum changes? Say the number of records in the Triadic Continuum increases to 1,657,999 and the number of transactions that occurred in Pennsylvania increased to 1,110,258. Using the same principle, one would divide the numerator 1,110,258 by 1,657,999, or 66% of the transactions now occur in Pennsylvania. As Peirce was saying, the probability is nothing more than the numerator divided by the denominator, at any given time.

You may have noticed that there is one other sentence in the above Peirce quote, which reads, "Now the expression in question names the numerator of the fraction, but omits to name the denominator." The "expression in question" refers back to the first sentence where Peirce says, "There are those to whom the idea of an unknown probability seems an absurdity." Here Peirce means that those who believe only in naive probability use just the numerator, the frequency of a specific kind of event, the number of times a coin is tossed or the number of possibilities of getting two aces in the hole. They don't concern themselves with the natural frequency of the totality of events in which the specific type of event can occur. They don't consider the overall experience as a factor in looking at probability. But that is exactly what Peirce and Mazzagatti are saying, that probability can be viewed as both naive and experiential.

Before continuing, let me summarize the criteria that I've been using to explain both naïve and experiential probability. While not precise or rigorous, the following table illustrates a few key criteria that each type of probability displays.

Naive Probability	Experiential Probability
Known, well-defined set of possibilities, events, or situations	Unknown set of possibilities, events, or situations
A finite set of possibilities	Presumably an infinite set of possibilities
Equal potential	Unequal potential
No specific context (no experience involved)	A specific context (relies on experience)
Static	Dynamic

Figure 12–2

Each of these criterions differentiates one type of probability from another, but it is the last one that I want to discuss next, that of the dynamic nature of the Triadic Continuum.

Dynamic Probability

Another name for experiential probability might be "dynamic probability," or probability that changes dynamically as the information from which the probability is calculated changes. Think of it this way: in traditional database structures, the data are gathered, organized, and then queried. As I've mentioned before, most often the data is historical, i.e., it has been gathered beforehand and is static; it doesn't change, nothing new comes into the mix until the next time the data structure is updated, which could be the next day, next week, or at the end of the quarter. Having the ability to dynamically organize and query data on the fly is a very important and significant feature. And, as you're fully aware by now, the Triadic Continuum is a dynamic data structure. The Triadic Continuum's ability to dynamically organize and query data is what we talk about when the phase "real-time queries" are suggested. This is made possible by the unique structure and the fact that the probabilities are calculated dynamically—so, as the data changes, so changes the probability—a probability based on the ever-changing experience in the world of incoming fast-moving data. Dynamic probability is truly something new in the world of real-time query of data structures.

Weaknesses of Other Data Structures

Two characteristics of the Triadic Continuum show its superiority over other types of data structures. First there is the concept of a static data structure versus a dynamic one, and second the idea of training the data structure versus having the structure actually learning the information. I've have already discussed the dynamic nature of the Triadic Continuum, but not the concept of training.

Many types of decision-making applications and data structures that might collectively be referred to as "knowledge databases," must be trained before they can be used. The term *training* is actually a slight misnomer; these structures are generally provided with what is called a "training set," which is simply data from the problem area. For example, in order to train a structure to allow it to be queried with questions regarding buying trends of male online shoppers, the structure must be loaded with historic transactional data that includes male shopper data. The concept of training is found in areas such as expert systems, neural networks, and Markov chains, among others. Often this training is accomplished in five steps before it can be used. The following five steps are from a paper on training neural networks, which I have generalized for this discussion:

1. Expose the structure to pre-existing data

2. Evaluate the data to generate output data based on the state of the information

3. Compare the generated output data with known correct data and evaluate the performance

4. Modify the state of the structure (including the probabilities) to improve performance

5. Test the performance of the modified structure and repeat as necessary[12]

One weakness of training accomplished in this manner is that the data is limited to the data available at the time of training, it is historical data and by now I'm sure you understand that that means that it is never current. Those using these types of data structures have gotten around this weakness by periodically updating the structure with the most recent history. However, the data is never streamed in real time. On the other hand, as you're aware, the Triadic Continuum does process streams of live data, as they are experienced. If you think of the way you learn, it's by experiencing live data, recording it into some form of neuronal structure in the brain, and then, hopefully retrieving it when needed. I say "hopefully" because as we all know, learning isn't that simple. Among others, the context in which the learning takes place and relevant examples are important in learning and retention. However, we can think of "learning" in the Triadic Continuum as a three-step process: experiencing the data, forming it into the structure of the Triadic Continuum of nodes and connexions, and then retrieving the information needed by querying the structure. If you refer back to the list above of the five steps of training other data structures, you will see that the main difference between learning in the Triadic Continuum and training in other data structures is the 4th step: Modify the state. What this means is that the owner of the traditional structure changes the probabilities in order to improve its performance. In other words, to make it more accurate and realistic the owner must manipulate the probabilities. I'm sure you know by now that the Triadic Continuum needs no probability manipulation, in fact, as explained earlier, the probabilities aren't determined until they need to be determined.

The second weakness of training is of under- or over-training. Under-training is fairly obvious. Provide data with too few instances of certain types of transactions, occurrences, or important data and there is not enough information to use to make accurate predictions. Over-training is a different story. The following explains the problems encountered when training a neural network.

> Overtraining occurs when a network has learned not only the basic mapping associated with input and output data, but also the subtle nuances and even the errors specific to the training set. If too much training occurs, the network only memorizes the training set and loses its ability to generalize to new data. The result is a network that performs well on the training set but performs poorly on out-of-sample test data and later during actual trading.[13]

There are, of course, workarounds for under and overtraining in these other types of structures, but with the Triadic Continuum, there is no need for workarounds—the data that goes in is the data that is used, answers to queries based on this data are as accurate as the data available.

As mentioned above, there are many other types of computational models that use probabilities. I mentioned three—neural networks, expert systems, and Markov Chains—but there are others that use similar paradigms. And, while widely different from the Triadic Continuum and each other, they were all designed to solve the problem of finding answers buried in large amounts of data. Neural networks, so named because they were originally designed to imitate what the designers believe, are the structure of the human brain, are comprised of interconnected groupings of nodes, or artificial neurons. An expert system is a data structure that contains some of the knowledge of a human expert. Queries are asked of the structure in order to determine answers to problems that generally only an expert in that area of study would know.

Markov chains, defined by Andrei Markov in the early 20th century, are a form of data structure that uses nodes, branches, and probabilities, to "model sequences of events where the probability of an event occurring depends upon the fact that a preceding event occurred."[14] Markov chains have been used extensively in the field of speech recognition where chains are constructed from large bodies of real speech data.

In the following example I don't plan to minimize what other data structures can or cannot do, but many of their perceived strengths and advantages are actually shortcomings when looked at in comparison to the Triadic Continuum. Also, in the next few pages I do simplify a complex topic quite a bit, but I'm not trying to minimize the worth of these other data structures, I'm simply trying to show how the dynamic nature of the Triadic Continuum and experiential probability lead to a structure that may very well be more like the actual network of neurons in a human brain than other structures that exist today. Let's use the Markov chain as an example.

Typically the way a Markov chain works is that data are passed into the structure through sets of inputs. From there, data are multiplied by weights, which have previously been assigned to each branch depending on data that was presented during a teaching stage. For example, assume that the nine records in the Bill and Tom furniture store dataset were taught. If need be, refer back to Figure 12–1 to refresh your memory. Bill is associated with six of the nine records, or 66% of the time the transaction is Bill's. On the other hand, Tom is responsible for 33% of the transactions. This is all well and good for as far as this goes, but nine records isn't a whole lot of data to go on. Let's say there were 9,000 records and Bill was still 66% and Tom 33%. So, during the teaching stage, 9,000 records are input with 66% associated with Bill and 33% associated with Tom. The chain might look something like the following.

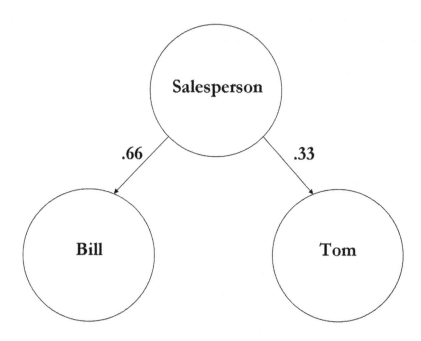

Figure 12–3

Because the chain was only taught the 9,000 records, the weights on the branches leading from the salesperson node reflect what was experienced during training, or, the likelihood is 66% that if a salesperson is involved it will be Bill. That's all the chain knows: what it has been taught. So, when the chain is queried, it will base it's responses on what it already knows. If the data changes and Tom has a fantastic two weeks during which he sells enough furniture to fill a 70-story office building, the chain will still tell only what it has been taught—Tom is associated with only 30% of the transactions. Even updating all the data in the structure means that all of the probabilities must be manually recalculated, a step that isn't necessary with the Triadic Continuum.

The dynamic nature of the Triadic Continuum, using experiential probability, is able to calculate the probability by what is being experienced, not what had been experienced at a previous static moment in time. So, as things begin to change and improve for Tom, the associated probability will change as well, all because the Triadic Continuum is dynamic and calculates probability as events are experienced. The way to think about this is that there is no probability until someone asks a question. Then and only then does a simple algorithm search for the nodes and divides the nominator by the denominator to determine the dynamic probability.

Mazzagatti believes that it's exactly what Peirce was referring to when he wrote,

> Probability applies to the question whether a specified kind of event will occur when certain predetermined conditions are fulfilled; and it is the ratio of the number of times in the long run in which that specified result would follow upon the fulfillment of those conditions to the total number of times in which those conditions were fulfilled in the course of experience. It essentially refers to a course of experience, or at least of real events; because mere possibilities are not capable of being counted. You can, for example, ask what the probability is that a given kind of object will be red, provided you define red sufficiently. It is simply the ratio of the number of objects of that kind that are red to the total number of objects of that kind.[15]

13

A Guess at the Riddle: Beyond the Practical Peirce

Phaneroscopy is the description of the phaneron; and by the phaneron I mean the collective total of all that is in any way or in any sense present to the mind, quite regardless of whether it corresponds to any real thing or not. Charles Peirce[1]

> *Mind is a field*
> *in which every kind of seed is sown.*
> *This mind-field can also be called*
> *"all the seeds."* Thich Nhat Hanh[2]

When Charles Peirce wrote "... the collective total of all that is in any way or in any sense present to the mind," in defining of the word "phaneron," he was attempting to define a branch of human thought that would explain the workings of the human mind. Mazzagatti believes that Peirce's theories of semiotics, pragmatism, and existential graphs were directed at bringing form to his idea of the phaneron as being able to explain the structure and function of the human mind. It can also be said that much of his writing in logic and mathematics was in support of this.

In talking about the phaneron and its importance to Peirce's overall work in the sciences and philosophy, Mazzagatti says that, "Peirce has left us signposts, and it is our job to fill in the rest of the puzzle." She believes that one of the proofs that he knew that his work was foundational comes from his plan for a proposed book that was, in his own words

> to make a philosophy like that of Aristotle, that is to say, to outline a theory so comprehensive that, for a long time to come, the entire work of human reason, in philosophy of every school and kind, in mathematics, in psychology, in

physical science, in history, in sociology, and in whatever other department there may be, shall appear as the filling up of its details.[3]

During the last 30 years of his life, Peirce planned to write this proposed book that would outline and explain much of this grand theory. In his notes he referred to the book as "A Guess at the Riddle" and one can sense its scope in an outline called "Plan of the Work."[4] One can also get a sense of how important Peirce believed it to be when he writes "And this book, if ever written, as it soon will be if I am in a situation to do it, will be one of the births of time."[5]

Because of a number of reasons, his book was never completed, but the outline is found in his papers. The book was to be divided into nine sections. One can get a sense of the grandeur of his thought when the titles and a brief synopsis of each section are read. The first section covered Peirce's concepts of firstness, secondness, thirdness followed by a section on the triad of reasoning. Following this, Peirce lists section three as the triad in metaphysics. In his own words he states that, "This chapter, one of the best, is to treat the theory of cognition."[6] And then, as if to show the vast scope of his thinking, he continues with sections on the triad in psychology, physiology, physics, sociology, biology, where he specially notes that in biology he will show "the true nature of the Darwinian hypothesis.[7] He finishes with the triad in theology.

To some, a scheme as grand as this may sound like the ranting of a madman, while to others it sounds like a work of incredible genius, and even those who revere Peirce's polymath abilities are often hesitant in praise of the enormity of scope and audacity of his genius.

In the introduction to his Peirce biography, *A Life*, Joseph Brent writes that Peirce scholar Max H. Fisch, "who spent fifty years in the dedicated study of Peirce's life and thought, offered a far more knowledgeable and even grander judgment of Peirce's achievements"[8] than others have. However, Brent notes that not even Fisch recognizes the vastness of Peirce's scheme. About Fisch, Brent writes

> He does not respond to the extraordinary daring, grand, and powerful vision which Peirce expressed in his intention "to outline a theory so comprehensive that ... the entire work of human reason ... shall appear as the filling up of its details.[9]

In the same paragraph, Brent continues

> Nor does he recognize the hubris manifest in Peirce's intention to make "the entire work of human reason" a string of footnotes to his own philosophical system.[10]

If what Brent means by hubris is overbearing presumption, Mazzagatti believes Brent's opinion shortsighted. She believes that Peirce knew that the triad was the answer to the questions of reasoning, cognition, as well as more far-ranging areas of human thought.

Mazzagatti also believes that when Peirce said that the Phaneron is "the collective total of all that is in any way or in any sense present to the mind,"[11] he meant a "rigorous mathematical "all" with his feet firmly in science."[12] As a software engineer and mathematician herself, she firmly believes that as a scientist and especially a mathematician Peirce used language in an unambiguously precise way. So, when he uses the word "all," he's not using it figuratively, but quite literally. Ask her and she will tell you that she believes that Peirce could see the Triadic Continuum in his mind's eye, and that all of what he did in the last years of his life was directed at explaining what he alone could see. For example, Mazzagatti believes that Peirce's existential graphs were an attempt to make visible to everyone all that is contained in the triadic continuum of the Phaneron. But, during the end of the 19th century and beginning of the 20th, Peirce was limited as to the methods he had available to illustrate and demonstrate what he saw. Had other technologies been available, such as computer software programming or database design, he may have had the tools he needed to explain his theories. Besides that, during the last 20 years of his life, Peirce was fending off the fallout of his poor social skills, his cavalier behavior to others, his and his wife's illnesses, and a lack of income that forced him to accept charity from his friends. Quite possibly, had he been surrounded by scientific peers in an academic setting rather than living in isolation in a cottage in rural Pennsylvania, he may have been able to finish the expanded outline of his book and seen the start of other scientists filling in the details; possibly not.

Based on his expansive and diverse knowledge of the sciences, Peirce was able to imagine to a degree what an understanding of the triad would bring to mankind. In his attempt to communicate his understanding, he fathered semiotics, the study of signs, defined Pragmatism, or Pragmaticism as he later called it, and developed existential graphs to graphically represent the contents of the Phaneron. But, his imagination could only take him so far, which leads us back to Mazzagatti.

In Mazzagatti's reinterpretation of Piece's seminal work, she has found a method to explain Peirce using computer and database theory and technology—to make him more "practical" if you will. However, this isn't to say that the computer data structure that Mazzagatti visualized and then invented is the end of the things that can be imagined through a more formal understanding of phaneroscopy; it may be just the beginning.

The remainder of this book covers those areas in which Mazzagatti and colleagues are able to imagine potential areas of interest in which this knowledge may have practical and theoretical uses. By no means is this a comprehensive list. As one becomes more involved with understanding the Triadic Continuum and it subtleties and elegance, more layers and depth are discovered.

Those Things Imaginable

Hopefully by this point in reading this book, you have a firm understanding that the data structure that Jane Mazzagatti invented is a viable potential structure with practical commercial application in the computer industry. If that's true then, at least in the computer industry, Peirce's work is not just theoretical, but highly practical; however, Mazzagatti believes that his work has practical applications in many other fields and areas.

Before going on, it might be helpful to mention that Mazzagatti views Peirce's Phaneron as the entire content of the mind, all that a person has experienced and observed as well as imagined and created mentally. She sees the Triadic Continuum, built of triads, as a model of the physical structure that that is the framework of the Phaneron, with its unique organization of nodes (neurons) and connexions (dendrites and axons). And, the simple, elegant way in which they are associated enables the data to be recorded into the structure (constructed) and quickly retrieved when needed.

The Importance of a Biological Structure

In his prophetic book, *On Intelligence*, Jeff Hawkins talks about his interest in the human brain and his quest to understand the state of the art in knowledge about human intelligence. He says that in 1986, as he was attempting to gain an understanding of the history of intelligence, he was drowning in details. He says that

> There was an unending supply of things to study and read about, but I was not gaining any clear understanding of how the whole brain actually worked or even what it did. This was because the field of neuroscience itself was awash in details. It still is. Thousands of research reports are published every year, but they tend to add to the heap rather than organize it. There's still no overall theory, no framework, explaining what your brain does and how it does it.[13]

And so it's been since Peirce's death in 1914, those that have come after have added observations and facts without providing an overall theory of reasoning and cognition. Mazzagatti, like Hawkins believes that without a clear picture of the physical structure, there's no way to understand the brain. She believes that the structure that Peirce saw and attempted to define and the structure that she rediscovered and is developing, as a computer data structure, is the elusive framework that many are trying to identify in the field of neurobiology.

Hawkins identifies three things he believes are essential to an understanding of the brain. The first is that "real brains process rapidly changing streams of information."[14] The second criterion is that feedback is important and that "feedback dominates most connections throughout the neocortex as well."[15] And the third is

> that any theory or model of the brain should account for the physical architecture of the brain. The neocortex is not a simple structure ... it is organized as a repeating hierarchy.[16]

In earlier chapters I have made the case that unlike other data structures, the Triadic Continuum is able to process data and information in a continuous, steady, and rapidly changing stream. The fundamental organization of the structure of nodes and connexions and the interaction between them is an indication of the mechanism of the Triadic Continuum. And, as you have seen in Chapters 3–5 the Triadic Continuum is a hierarchical structure organized in multiple levels of hierarchies that are created from recording sequences of data. However, it is not our intent in this book to prove conclusively that the Triadic Continuum fulfils all of these criteria. Rather, it is our intention to bring to your attention that it is highly likely that the structure of the Triadic Continuum is a model that should be investigated in the quest to discover the structure of the reasoning in the human brain. As Peirce believed, it will be left to others with specialized knowledge in many fields to fill in the gaps and match the known facts with this theory of a dynamic structure.

Thinking Strategies

To this point in this book, all I've really done is to explain what the Triadic Continuum is and how it is constructed. However, recently Mazzagatti and colleague Jane Claar have been spending time on the problem of thinking strategies. They believe that if the Triadic Continuum is the structure and organizing framework of the brain that there must be strategies that exist that are used to facilitate the retrieval of needed information quickly and efficiently. Mazzagatti and Claar call these "thinking strategies" or "thinking algorithms" in the context of the Triadic Continuum as a computer data structure.

Mazzagatti thinks that there is probably a small number of very abstract thinking strategies that the brain uses to process and retrieve information in a K, once a neuron (node) is formed—possibly a strategy for retrieving information that has been previously been experienced and another for associating old and new information. Quite possibly there are strategies for guessing and strategies for logical thinking.

Logical thinking is an interesting example. Mazzagatti has been toying with the notion that as we learn, various types of signs may be connected in the Triadic Continuum by, among other ways, context and classification (e.g., words, nouns, categories, etc.). For example, remember when you were in elementary school and you were memorizing the parts of speech and learning which words were nouns and verbs and so on? Mazzagatti thinks that as you learn these words and their meanings in the context of grammar that you eventually associate a "classifier" with a group of words, a word or idea that brings all of these words into one specific context. So, for example, once you have learned that the word "dog" is a noun and that "cat" is also a noun, that there is an additional connexion between dog and cat through the context of the classifier "nouns." Of course, there are other associations as well, such as cats and dogs have four legs and are furry, among others.

This isn't an entirely new idea. Hawkins, in *On Intelligence* talks about "sequences of sequences." Hawkins believes that,

As information moves up from primary sensory regions to the higher levels, we see fewer and fewer changes over time.[17] Regions store these songlike sequences about anything and everything: the sound of surf crashing on the beach, your mother's face, the path from your home to the corner store, how to spell the word "popcorn," how to shuffle a deck of cards.

We have names for songs, and in a similar fashion each cortical region has a name for each sequence it knows. This "name" is a group of cells whose collective firing represents the set of objects in the sequence.[18]

In the first paragraph above, Hawkins is describing the sequences of the Triadic Continuum, where each sequence is a "songlike sequence about anything and everything."[19] In the second paragraph, he is describing the sequences of known associations in the Triadic Continuum—things that have been committed to memory or habit, which have been recorded in the Triadic Continuum as a new sequence of data, able to be used and reused almost indefinitely, such as the fact that "cat" and "dog" are grammatically associated as the part of speech called a noun.

Hawkins also says that these predictable sequences are collapsed into "'named objects'" at each region in our hierarchy."[20] Today, Mazzagatti and Claar are writing software algorithms to define these "named objects." They have created special end-of-thought (EOT) nodes to represent these objects and programs to quickly access them. This makes retrieval of data in the Triadic Continuum computer data structure extremely quick. For example, after associating the EOT node "nouns" with all of the words that are nouns in a data structure, finding all items that are nouns, the computer query must only retrieve a single node to determine the total number of nouns in the data structure. Plus, creating a list of all the nouns is quicker because the query must only traverse the connexions from the "noun EOT" backward to the nodes for cat, dog, and all other nouns in the structure.

While today Mazzagatti may be writing code to define these named objects, she continuously points out that Peirce said that everything is in the structure. So, she believes, she will eventually incorporate all of these categorical associations (named objects) into the structure of the Triadic Continuum itself, as well as all of the thinking strategies she uncovers, thus conforming to Peirce's conviction that "all that is in any way or in any sense present to the mind"[21] be a part of the structure.

What this idea of named objects might mean to the idea of thinking strategies becomes quite clear with a simple, yet very persuasive example using grammar, simple logic, and the "ordinary syllogism:

> All men are mortal,
> Elijah was a man;
> Therefore, Elijah was mortal."[22]

Generally, a syllogism consists of three parts, "the major premise, the minor premise, and the conclusion."[23] Given the major and minor premise, the mind must determine the conclusion. Mazzagatti believes that there is a strategy for evaluating evidence such as the major and minor premises in order to determine the logical conclusion. To see how this might work, we need to put the major and minor premises into a Triadic Continuum as shown in Figure 13–1. Notice that the major premise of the above syllogism is labeled (path 10) and the minor premise is labeled (path 15).

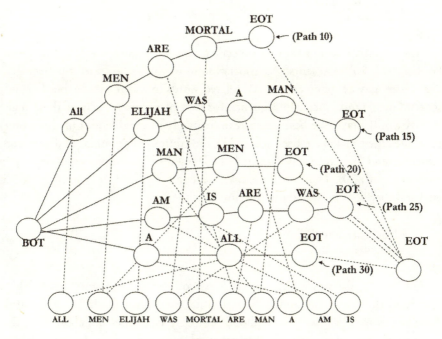

Figure 13–1

As explained above, it is Mazzagatti's theory that words and phrases have many associations in the Triadic Continuum depending on the context in which they are learned and used. Using the "All men are mortal" syllogism, you may notice that there are a number of associations between the words in the major and minor premise. For example the words "are" and "was" may be associated as tenses of the verb "to be." Notice sequence (path 25) in Figure 13–1, which is made up of nodes (signs) related because they are forms of the verb "to be." In theory, these sequences of word relationships most likely have been learned previously.

In Mazzagatti's theory, an evidence gathering strategy may work like this. First, words that are somehow associated are in a sense equal and therefore cancel one another out. Mazzagatti explains this in terms of the general algebraic process of canceling out common factors. For example, because they both are part of a named object sequence (i.e., tenses of the verb "to be"), the word "are" in the major premise cancels out the word "was" in the minor premise, leaving us with:

> All men ~~are~~ mortal,
> Elijah ~~was~~ a man;

Next, another association is cancelled out. In Figure 13–1 the sequence labeled (path 20) represents and association of words dealing with the male gender. There may be many other male-related words in this sequence, but I've only shown "man" and "men" in sequence for ease of viewing. Each of these male-related words may have been learned individually in childhood, but then sometime later they may have been learned in the context of grammar and verb construction and therefore have formed the named object sequence as shown in sequence (path 20). That being the case, man and men obviously must be associated and therefore cancelled out, leaving us with:

> All ~~men~~ ~~are~~ mortal,
> Elijah ~~was~~ a ~~man~~;

And finally, the words "a" and "all." As you can see in Figure 13–1, I have associated the words "a" and "all" in a sequence labeled (path 30). Of course, these words were learned in childhood, but only later does the child learn that these words may also represent mathematical concepts as well. In mathematics, the word "all" represents the entire known set of elements, while "a" represents one element in a set. So, at sometime in a person's life the concept of these two words as a mathematical concept are learned and form a special sequence in the Phaneron. Again, if Mazzagatti's theory holds true, the words "all" and "a" cancel each other out, leaving us with:

> All ~~men~~ ~~are~~ **mortal**,
> **Elijah** ~~was~~ ~~a~~ ~~man~~;

The two remaining words "Mortal" and "Elijah" make up those that commonly conclude this syllogism—"Therefore, Elijah was mortal."[24]

While this example may be a very simple, if this is actually the way the brain operates, it makes sense that it should be simple and elegant. In *On Intelligence*, Hawkins spends a great deal of pages explaining why the field of Artificial Intelligence (AI), as it stands today, will never produce a brain-like computer. Basically, he says that, practitioners of AI have spent their time programming human/brain-like behaviors into computers instead of attempting to discover the structure of the brain. He states that

> The answer is the brain doesn't "compute" the answers to problems; it retrieves the answers from memory. In essence, the answers were stored in memory a long time ago. It only takes a few steps to retrieve something from memory.[25]

Mazzagatti is the first to agree, "This is exactly what Peirce was saying, everything that is stored in the Phaneron and when needed it only takes a few steps to retrieve it."[26] And, for Mazzagatti, it's now just a matter of discovering the strategies the brain uses to retrieve each type of information it needs. She and Claar admit that they haven't yet discovered the really abstract strategies, but they believe that they will be related to abstract thinking behaviors.

The Brain as Prediction Engine

Returning again to *On Intelligence*, Hawkins' theory can be summarized by the statement that the "remarkably uniform arrangement of cortical tissue reflects a single principle or algorithm which underlies all cortical information processing.[27] As Hawkins explains, this "memory-prediction framework" enables the brain to process information by making predictions about a current situation or experience by what has been previously experienced. In other words, based on previously stored memories, the brain makes predictions about the current observed experience. Hawkins uses a thought experiment, called the "altered door" experiment to explain how the brain makes predictions about the world around us. In the experiment, Hawkins asks what would happen if someone secretly changed the front door to your home or apartment just a little bit, by adding a few ounces to its weight or moving the door knob an inch to the left or right, or some other non-obvious change. When you came home and tried to use it, you would quickly know that something is different. He explains that you would notice the change very quickly because your brain

> makes low-level sensory predictions about what it expects to see, hear, and feel in every given moment, and it does so in parallel. All regions of your neocortex are simultaneously trying to predict what their next experience will be. Visual areas make predictions about edges, shapes, objects, locations, and motions. Auditory areas make predictions about tones, direction to source, and pattern of sound. Somatosensory areas make predictions about touch, texture, contour, and temperature.

> Prediction" means that the neurons involved in sensing your door become active in advance of them actually receiving sensory input. When the sensory input does arrive, it is compared with what is expected. As you approach the door, your cortex is forming a slew of predictions based on past experiences.[28]

To explain this in terms of what you already know about the Triadic Continuum, I'll reuse an example I used in the last chapter, when I explained experiential probability. Remember the example of the young child, who upon her first encounter with a black dog is bitten. The next time she encounters a black dog, her brain quickly makes a prediction based on the state of experiential probability that exists at that moment. In this case the experiential probability is 100% and she will of course be quite reticent of being near the dog. However, with a parent's reassuring words, if she is able to meet the challenge and make the encounter, the experiential probability drops to 50% and continues to decrease each time she meets and is not harassed by a black dog. Thereafter, each time she encounters a black dog, the prediction algorithm that the brain uses will search the structure of the brain reassessing the experiential probabilities of being bitten. In each encounter when the dog does not bite her, a new memory is created, one where black dogs don't bite.

There must be thousands of predictions made each minute as we encounter all different types of sensory stimuli, situations, and experiences as we make our way through our exterior physical world as well as our own interior world of thought, ideas and imagination. And it is Mazzagatti's theory that the unique structure of the Triadic Continuum is so organized as to enable this rapid crisscrossing of the structure starting from previous known concepts, signs, and other memories.

Natural Selection

Besides the enormous impact the Triadic Continuum will have on neurobiology, other areas of biology will also be influenced. One of the most interesting areas is that of Darwinian Natural Selection. Earlier in this chapter I mentioned that one of the planned chapters in Peirce's book was to deal with the theory of Natural Selection and "the true nature of the Darwinian hypothesis.[29] What could Peirce have meant by the true nature of Natural Selection? The Nobel Prize winning scientist and author of a number of books on the brain, the mind, and intelligence, Gerald M. Edelman has stated that

> There must be ways to put the mind back into nature that are concordant with how it got there in the first place. These ways must heed what we have learned from the theory of evolution. In the course of evolution, bodies came to have minds. But it is not enough to say that the mind is embodied: one must say how. To do that we have to take a look at the brain and the nervous system and at the structural and functional problems they present.[30]

In Edelman's influential 1992 book, *Bright Air, Brilliant Fire: On the Matter of the Mind,* he uses a term, that after reading the book you now have in your hands, will seem familiar. The term is "maps" and Edelman uses it in explaining the structure of the neurons of the brain. He says

> Neurons come in a variety of shapes, and the shape determines in part how a neuron links up with others to form the neuroanatomy of a given brain area. Neurons can be anatomically arranged in many ways and are sometimes disposed into maps. Mapping is an important principle in complex brains. Maps relate points on the two-dimensional receptor sheets of the body (such as the skin or the retina of the eye) to corresponding points on the sheets making up the brains.[31]

One can see the correspondence to these maps and the Triadic Continuum. Mazzagatti conjectures that the maps in the retina of the eye, for example, contain a Triadic Continuum that records images, and a corresponding one in the brain's visual cortex. In terms of anatomy, physiology, embryology and evolution this makes sense. Why create a different structure than one that is already created? Biologically speaking that makes no sense at all. The simple and elegant thing for evolution to do is to reuse existing structures, but in a more sophisticated way.

In *Bright Air, Brilliant Fire*, Edelman explains the basic tenets of his theory called the theory of neuronal group selection (TNGS), originally described in his 1987 book entitled *Neural Darwinism: The Theory of Neuronal Group Selection*. Edelman theorizes that human intelligence and consciousness can be explained by Darwinian Selection. Edelman's TNGS also suggests that

> the brain constructs maps of its *own* activities, not just of external stimuli, as in perception. According to the theory, the brain areas responsible for concept formation contain structures that categorize, discriminate, and recombine the various brain activities occurring *in different kinds of global mappings*.[32] (Italics Edelman)

These ideas sound much like the characteristics of the Triadic Continuum that I have discussed and believe, as does Mazzagatti, that Peirce also accepted. No one knows exactly what Peirce was planning to write in the section of his book on the Darwinian hypothesis, but it may have been the precursor to Edelman's theory with emphasis on his own theory of signs. Unless there are Peirce manuscript pages unaccounted for, we'll never know.

Related Fields

With a basic understanding of the structure of the human brain, many other related areas of interest and specialization will of course be impacted. It should be obvious that fields such as biology, psychology, linguistics, learning theory, as well as computer programming have a lot to gain from an understanding of the Triadic Continuum. As mentioned earlier, Mazzagatti, with her diverse background in mathematics, educational psychology, and computer science, sees many of the interactions and connectedness among diverse disciplines. As I write this, she is preparing to present papers on the Triadic Continuum at conferences in different diverse disciplines.

One of the fields that Mazzagatti believes will be strongly impacted is in computer programming. In 1945, John Von Neumann, one of the early pioneers of the computer age, developed the concept that computers need not be specifically hard-wired to perform every task. Instead, using a method called "shared-program technique," the computer hardware could be simple and the instructions for the tasks it is to perform would be in the form of a shared "program." As computer languages began to be developed, the skill of the human programmer was in writing computer instructions (code) that accomplished more and more complex tasks, from simple calculations to today's ever-complex software programs. From the early days of programming until the present, a rule of thumb for the programming community has been what is called, "lines of code." Lines of code, as its name implies is a count of the number of lines of code in a given program, a corollary being that the more lines of code it has, the more mature the software application. This has been the way it's been—up until now. Mazzagatti believes that one implementation of the Triadic Continuum will be as a tool to create computer applications. However, instead of programming lines of code, people will be able to type experiential information into a Triadic Continuum that already contains the necessary information and strategies to build, traverse, and query the structure and to output applications that can be used on other computers, maybe even computers designed for use solely with a Triadic Continuum. So, instead of more and more lines of code to create a software application, it will take none—in reality there is no coding, simply a Triadic Continuum learning from the data being typed or streamed into it from a human wanting to create a computer application. Mazzagatti likes to tell a story about a high-level software engineer from a very large computer company, you know the company, the one whose name is synonymous with computer hardware. Upon listening to Mazzagatti's presentation on the Triadic Continuum he asked her how many lines of code it contained. Sensing that he equated the greater number of lines of code with a more mature product, she not only told him the number of lines of code to construct nodes, traverse connexions, and formulates strategies to find results, but also the number of lines of code for all of the applications surrounding the structure. So she told him that there were hundreds of thousands lines of code, which seemed to satisfy his curiosity that the application was in its adolescence, not a baby, but not quite grown. Mazzagatti knew that if she told him the truth that her original code to build and traverse the structure and formulate answers to questions was less than a thousand lines of code that he and his colleagues would have laughed and told her it was still immature.

And here's the rub, as Mazzagatti and her colleagues continue to work on the computer structure implantation of the Triadic Continuum, they continue to find ways to put more and more of the logic directly into the structure, without code, so that the necessary instructions are an integral part of the structure and not a separate entity that interacts with the structure as does the software surrounding a traditional data structure, be it a simple table, a sophisticated data cube, or a complex neural network. This concept is not new in the computer field. The challenge has always been between the size of the data structure and the amount of coded algorithms. How much information to place in the data structure is balanced against how much coding is needed to access the information. That has been the way it's always been; lists, tables, arrays, and indexes are developed to try and limit the amount of code. But it's been unsuccessful until the Triadic Continuum. With the Triadic Continuum the K replaces both the code and the data structure. Everything is in the Triadic Continuum except for a few functional algorithms.

Even if we were to stop at computers and data structures, the Triadic Continuum would be a revolutionary idea. But add to that the theory that this structure is possibly the structure of the human brain with implications in neurobiology, psychology, linguistics, and learning theory, among many others and you can begin to see why Peirce believed that whole new fields of study would emerge and old fields will connect and show how different fields are related. Peirce saw this when he stated the argument for completing the work started in his proposed book. In his notes he says that work will be conducted

> in a sort of game of "follow-my-leader" from one field of thought into another. Their importance was originally brought home to me in the study of logic, where they play so remarkable a part that I was led to look for them in psychology. Finding them there again, I could not help asking myself whether they did not enter into the physiology of the nervous system. By drawing a little on hypothesis, I succeeded in detecting them there; and then the question naturally came how they would appear in the theory of protoplasm in general.[33]

Final Thoughts

Over the last few years as I've interviewed Mazzagatti and talked with her about the implications of the Triadic Continuum, the possibility that she might be right in believing that she has rediscovered the structure, storage mechanism, and memory processes of the human brain has often kept me awake at night. However, as impressive as her possible accomplishment might be, many of us have also spent time thinking about other implications of the Triadic Continuum. Sometimes the implications are directly related to things we have already thought about, but at other times they aren't. So, in ending this book I'd like to leave you with some final thoughts that deal with a few of these other implications.

The first one deals with the idea of the fragmented nature of our knowledge of the external world of our senses as well as the internal world of our imagination. I've often felt that there must be some connection between the sciences and the rest of our knowledge and the artifacts of our creativity. So, it was with delight that in 1998 I read a book by biologist Edward O. Wilson entitled *Consilience: The Unity of Knowledge.* In the opening chapters, Wilson talks about "the ongoing fragmentation of knowledge and the resulting chaos in philosophy are not reflections of the real world but artifacts of scholarship."[34] Wilson imagines that it is possible that knowledge in the sciences and the humanities are synergistic and uses the term "consilience" to mean a "jumping together" of knowledge. While intellectually moved by the imaginative scope of this book, it felt as though something was missing—to me it needed a framework in which it might be possible. Not until I worked with Mazzagatti and understood the deeper implications of the Triadic Continuum did I sense that Wilson's consilience might actually be able to be proven scientifically.

It's likely that had Peirce been alive and after reading Wilson's book, he would have begun a correspondence, as he was often likely to do with someone whose ideas interested him. I also believe that Peirce would have felt that his own work fit nicely into Wilson's premise and that it was a validation of Peirce's own theories. I do believe that Peirce's theories and Mazzagatti's invention of the mechanism and processing of the Triadic Continuum can be a stepping stone to a true understanding of Wilson's consilience of knowledge.

The second thought is one that has been with me since college and it deals with the principle of Occam's Razor. Commonly attributed to the 14th century Franciscan friar William of Ockham, I remember my developmental biology professor explaining it as a principle, which is stated as, given any set of facts, the simplest explanation is the best.[35] The professor explained that often the simplest theory, process, or mechanism in nature is the one that is eventually found to be true. After reading the following excerpt from a book entitled *What Is Mind* by computer scientist and physicist Eric Baum I'm pretty sure Occam's Razor is taught to students in other scientific fields as well as biology

> Occam's Razor underlies all of science. It is, for example, the way in which
> physicists come to their small collection of simple laws that fundamentally
> explain all physical phenomena, how chemists arrive at the periodic table, why
> biologists believe in heredity. Newton's laws, for example, are simple in the
> sense that they can be written down on a single page, yet they explain a vast
> number of physical experiments and phenomena.[36]

I don't exactly remember the context in which my professor introduced me to
Occam's Razor, but I do remember thinking that it was one of those ideas that
felt inherently true. And, as I've grown older, I realize that it also fits into my
overall worldview. It's not that I'm not allowing for complexity, it's that I've
noticed that most ideas, concepts, and even human relationships are at the core
much more simple than complex. So it was interesting to read Baum say that it
was the claim of his book "that Occam's Razor (as generalized and extended) is
the basis of the mind itself."[37] When I read that, it immediately brought to mind
two words that I have used throughout this book: "simple" and "elegant." My use
of these words in this book when talking about the Triadic Continuum has not
been accidental. As you understand how the structure of the Triadic Continuum
works, you realize just how really simple it is; and by simple I don't meant trivial,
I mean not complex. Whenever I've discussed the Triadic Continuum with Mazzagatti or worked with other team members to write the patents, I've gone
through two noticeable stages. At first I was overwhelmed by the seeming complexity of what they were explaining, but then after thinking about it, I've found
that at its heart the concept was actually very simple, and elegant in its simplicity.
You just need to go back to the earlier chapters on how the Triadic Continuum is
constructed and how knowledge is realized within the structure to see just how
elegantly simple this structure is.

So, with my background and interest in biology, it was only a matter of time
before I began discussing with Mazzagatti my own ideas about simplicity versus
complexity, neuronal development, and whether the structure of the Triadic
Continuum might indeed be the organizing structure and mechanism of the
brain. Our conversations have led us to discuss and theorize on the evolutionary
development of the neuronal structure of the brain—to speculate, not as profes-
sional scientists in the field of developmental biology or neurobiology, but as dev-
otees of science and amateur theorists. We realize that the brain is complex, but
we also believe that there is a strong possibility that the evolution, development
of the neural pathways, and processing of the brain may follow Occam's Razor
and be formed and operate through a non complex structure and mechanism as

proposed in the model of the Triadic Continuum. It is possible to believe that the evolution and development of the neuronal pathway may have been accomplished through a series of incremental modifications—some of which resulted in increased intelligence and others that did not. I can almost see the transition from a primitive neural structure to a branching of neurons where chemical and electrical messages connect sensory receptors to a few associated neurons as with the sensory and elemental nodes of a Triadic Continuum, where all that must be developed (evolved) are a set number of chemical or electrical strategies to build memories, and others to traverse the structure. Let's posit that it is possible that during the evolution of the development of the neuronal pathways that the simplest mechanism was used to associate one neuron in a particular event with another. It is feasible to accept that the simple connection of neurons could be selected rather than a more complicated one. So picture a neuron that is involved in a single memory with only three things it needs to "remember"—one connection from the sensory receptor at the site of the incoming stimuli, one to the neuron that proceeds it in the memory structure, and one to the neuron that continues or ends the sequence of stimuli in the memory. Only three associations for each neuron in a single sequence associated with any individual given memory. These are some of the ideas that others may someday extend, modify, refine, and ultimately prove.

Things Unimaginable

I'd like to end the book by talking about those things that Mazzagatti calls "those things unimaginable." When I ask her about those unimaginable things that the Triadic Continuum may someday be able to do, Mazzagatti shifts between pensive and animated. On the one hand she can see things that may seem today like science fiction, but on the other hand she knows that it will take time to get there—new theories that are this radical, and this elegantly simple often take time to be recognized for what they really are. If you ask her, she's willing to tell you that from the very beginning she's seen the structure of the Triadic Continuum as a model of the cognitive function of the human brain and the computer data structure as a way to implementation this model so others could see a practical implementation of her thoughts. Half of her time these days is spent implementing the computer application of the Triadic Continuum and the other half is spent in pure blue-sky research, which often takes the form of sitting and thinking and then discussing unimaginable ideas with Claar and other colleagues.

Mazzagatti says that in the middle of the night she is often unable to sleep because of what she calls "triadomania," which she defines as an affliction that comes over those who begin to understand the myriad implications of the Triadic Continuum. Interestingly enough, Peirce used a similar term "triadomany,"[38] to mean his predilection for things in threes. Mazzagatti's late night musings often lead her in the direction of the unimaginable implications of the Triadic Continuum as a model of the structure of the brain. Her musings are often a mixture of mathematics, neurobiology, computer science, and images and ideas from her favorite television program, "Star Trek." More than once she's used the android life-form, Commander Data from the television program, *Star Trek: The Next Generation*, to illustrate the potential to build a Triadic Continuum that contains the learning and thinking strategies, as well as the ability to learn new experiences and form new sequences within its artificial (positronic) neural structure. Mazzagatti believes in the potential to build an artificial life form that is aware and sentient because of its Triadic Continuum is filled with observations, experiences, and learning, thinking, and problem-solving strategies. While the construction of the body may be artificial, if she's correct, the composition of the brain will be more natural than artificial; hence, she believes, the Triadic Continuum may usher in the beginning of non-living Natural Intelligence and the end of Artificial Intelligence. She, like Peirce, is willing to put her ideas and theories into the hands of others so that she may see, in her lifetime, some of the seemingly unlimited unimaginable possibilities of the Triadic Continuum. Or, as she says, she has no choice, there's just too much to study and accomplish; the universe of areas that the Triadic Continuum touch are just too huge for a single person to uncover in a single lifetime.

Notes

The majority of the Peirce quotes are from the InteLex CD-ROM version of *The Collected Papers of Charles Sanders Peirce*. I used the standard notation used by those referencing the *Collected Papers*, which is, CP X.YYY, where X represents the volume number and YYY the paragraph number within the volume. For example, CP 1.221 is from paragraph number 221 within Volume 1.

Preface

1. CP 1.221

2. CP 8.259

3. CP 5.365

Chapter 1

1. CP1.7

2. CP1.239

3. Robert Burch. "Charles Sanders Peirce," *The Stanford Encyclopedia of Philosophy (Fall 2006 Edition)*, Edward N. Zalta (ed.), http://plato.stanford.edu/archives/fall2006/entries/peirce/ (accessed February 23, 2007)

4. Bertrand Russell and Paul Foulkes. "Wisdom of the West: A Historical Survey of Western Philosophy in Its Social and Political Setting," *International Affairs*. 37 (2), (1961): 207.

5. Max Fisch. *Studies in the Philosophy of Charles Sanders Peirce*. Edward C. Moore and Richard Robin (eds.) (University of Massachusetts Press, 1964), 486.

6. Kenneth Ketner. "RE: The "Practical Peirce," 18 February 2007, email (20 February 2007).

7. Joseph Brent. *Charles Sanders Peirce: A Life*. (Indiana University Press, 1993) 54.

8. "About us," The Office of Coast Survey, http://chartmaker.ncd.noaa.gov/staff/aboutus.htm, (accessed February 16, 2007).

9. "Welcome to Geodesy," NOAA National Ocean Service Education, http://www.oceanservice.noaa.gov/education/kits/geodesy/welcome.html (accessed February 16, 2007).

10. Brent, 137.

11. R. M. Martin, ed. *Studies in the Scientific and Mathematical Philosophy of Charles Sanders Peirce: Essays by Carolyn Eisele*. (The Hague: Mouton Publishers, 1979), 1.

12. CP 1:3

13. CP 7:65

14. Martin. 3.

15. "Charles Sanders Peirce," NOAA History, http://www.history.noaa.gov/giants/peirce.html (accessed February 16, 2007).

16. Martin. 2.

17. Kenneth L Ketner, "The Early History of Computer Design: Charles Sanders Peirce and Marquand's Logical Machines," *The Princeton University Library Chronicle*. 45 (3), (1984): 211.

18. CP 8:37

19. Carolyn Eisele, ed. *The New Elements of Mathematics by Charles S. Peirce*. (The Hague: Mouton & Co. B. V.) 1976. 1.

20. Carolyn Eisele, ed. *Historical Perspectives on Peirce's Logic of Science*. (Berlin: Walter de Gruyter and Co.) 1985. 5.

21. Eisele. *Historical Perspectives*. 306.

22. CP 5:411

23. CP 5:412

24. Martin. 8.

25. CP 8.110

26. CP 1:404

27. CP 8.213

28. Luis Ramirez. "*L* 67: Charles S. Peirce to Mario Calderoni on Pragmaticism (1905)," The Peirce Studies Group, 6 February 2006, http://www.unav.es/gep/LetterCalderoniEn.html. Accessed 2/23/07. On a transcribed copy of Peirce's letter to Mario Calderoni found online, Luis Ramirez, who transcribed and translated this letter indicated in parentheses that the word "riddle" in the paragraph cited refers to "of human existence, conduct, and thinking, and their relation to God and Nature." Professor Sara Barrena, of the University of Navarra, Pamplona, Spain helped clear up this issue.

29. Albert Atkin, "Peirce's Theory of Signs," *The Stanford Encyclopedia of Philosophy (Winter 2006 Edition)*, Edward N. Zalta (ed.), http://plato.stanford.edu/archives/win2006/entries/peirce-semiotics/ (accessed February 23, 2007).

30. Atkins. (accessed February 23, 2007).

31. Wikipedia contributors, "Semiotics," *Wikipedia, The Free Encyclopedia,* http://en.wikipedia.org/w/index.php?title=Semiotics&oldid=113862117 (accessed February 23, 2007).

32. Ramirez (accessed February 25, 2007).

33. Atkins. (accessed February 23, 2007).

34. Charles S. Hardwick, ed. *Semiotic and Significs.* 2nd Edition. (Elsah, Illinois: The Press of Asibe Associates, 2001). 85.

35. Atkins. (accessed February 23, 2007).

36. CP 5: 283

37. Jane Mazzagatti. 12 December 2006.

38. Martin, R. M (Ed.) Eisele. Page 7. Quote as part of article by the Maynard Institute. http://www.maynardije.org. (accessed February 20, 2007).

39. Allport, Gordon. *The Nature of Prejudice*. (New York: Addison-Wesley Publishing Company, 1954). 20.

40. CP 3.328

41. Wikipedia contributors, "Logic of relatives," *Wikipedia, The Free Encyclopedia,* http://en.wikipedia.org/w/index.php?title=Logic_of_relatives&oldid=112466839 (Accessed February 1, 2007).

42. Carolyn Eisele, ed. The *New Elements of Mathematics* (The Hague: Mouton Publishers, 1976) 4, 47–48.

43. John F. Sowa. "Existential Graphs. MS 514 by Charles Sanders Peirce with commentary by John F. Sowa." http://www.jfsowa.com/peirce/ms514.htm (Accessed February 12, 2007).

44. Martin. 3.

45. Wikipedia contributors, "Existential graph," *Wikipedia, The Free Encyclopedia,* http://en.wikipedia.org/w/index.php?title=Existential_graph&oldid=101805114. (Accessed February 23, 2007.

46. CP 4. 582

47. CP 4.8

48. CP 4.11

49. ____ "A World of Conceptual Graphs," http://conceptualgraphs.org (accessed March 2, 2007)

50. CP 8.385

51. Jaime Nubiola,. "Walter Percy and Charles S. Peirce: Abduction and Language,". Paper presented at the 6th Congress of the International Association for Semiotic Studies (IASS), Mexico, 1997. An English version of the paper

is found at http://user.uni-frankford.de/~wirth/texte/nubiola.htm (Accessed February 24, 2007).

52. Nubiola.

53. Charles Hartshorne and Paul Weiss, eds. "Introduction," *Collected Papers of Charles Sanders Peirce.* (Harvard University Press. 1932) Volume 2.

54. CP 3.470

55. CP 1.288—CP 1.291

56. ____ "Methods: Overview of Primary Materials." *The Peirce Edition Project.* http://iupui.edu/~peirce/writings/methodx.htm (Accessed February 25, 2007).

57. ____ "The Singular Experience of Peirce Biographer," *Arisbe. The Peirce Gateway.* http://members.door. net/arisbe/menu/library/aboutcsp/brent/singular.htm (Accessed February 25, 2007)

58. Peirce. Manuscript 507, page 3. Located on http://www.unav.es/gep/Port/ ms507/3.html (Accessed 6, 2007). bMS Am 1632 (2). By permission of Houghton Library, Harvard University

Chapter 2

1. CP 6.188

2. Fred Reed, interview by John Zuchero, taped and transcribed on 19 April 1999.

3. John Dewey, *Logic: The Theory of Inquiry.* (New York: Henry Holt and Company, 1938) 23.

4. Dewey. iii.

5. Dewey. 9.

6. ____ "John Dewey (1859–1952)," *The Internet Encyclopedia of Philosophy*, 2006. http://www.iep.utm.edu/d/dewey.htm (accessed 16 Nov 2005).

7. ____ "John Dewey (1859–1952)," *The Internet Encyclopedia of Philosophy*, 2006. http://www.iep.utm.edu/d/dewey.htm (accessed 16 Nov 2005).

8. ____ "John Dewey (1859–1952)," *The Internet Encyclopedia of Philosophy*, 2006. http://www.iep.utm.edu/d/dewey.htm (accessed 16 Nov 2005).

9. A. G. Dale, N. Dale, and E. D. Pendergraft, "A Programming System for Automatic Classification with Applications in Linguistic and Information Retrieval Research" (The Defense Technical Information Center 1964), http://www.dtic.mil (accessed 12 Dec 2006) and W. P. Lehmann and E. D. Pendergraft, "Linguistic Information Processing Study and Dynamic Adaptive Data Base Management Study" (The Defense Technical Information Center 1968), http://www.dtic.mil (accessed 12 Dec 2006).

10. Vern Blunk, interview by John Zuchero, taped and transcribed on 10 June 1999. This is taken from an interview I conducted with Mr. Blunk, who was the leader of the Unisys R&D team during the late 1990s. Unless otherwise indicated, his comments are based on his recollections of incidents. Some comments are based on emails he saved from the time he was leading the project.

11. Norm Hirst "The Autognome vs. Computers," Fax dated 9 October 1996). 2.

12. Eugene Pendergraft,. "Autognome Design Specification." (Creative Intelligence Incorporated, 26 October 1994). Unpublished.

13. Eugene Pendergraft,. "The Future's Voice: Intelligence Based on Pragmatic Logic." (Creative Intelligence Incorporated, June 1993). Unpublished.

14. Charles Peirce, "Logical Machines," *American Journal of Psychology*, 1 (1887): 1, 165–170

Chapter 3

1. Edgar F. Codd, "Normalized Data Base Structure: A Brief Tutorial." *Proc. 1971 ACM SIGFIDET Workshop on Data Description, Access, and Control*, San Diego, Calif. (November 11th-12th, 1971).

2. Wikipedia contributors, "Punch card," *Wikipedia, The Free Encyclopedia,* http://en.wikipedia.org/w/index.php?title=Punch_card&oldid=87442359. (accessed 29 Sep 2006).

3. Wikipedia contributors, "Linked list," *Wikipedia, The Free Encyclopedia,* http://en.wikipedia.org/w/index.php?title=Linked_list&oldid=111524335 (accessed 29 Sep 2006).

4. "Relational Database." WhatIs.com, The Technology Online Dictionary. http://searchoracle.techtarget.com/sDefinition/0,sid41_gci212885,00.html (accessed 29 Sep 2006).

5. "Relational Database."

6. Wikipedia contributors, "SQL," *Wikipedia, The Free Encyclopedia,* http://en.wikipedia.org/w/index.php?title=SQL&oldid=112815810 (accessed 29 Sep 2006

7. Robin Bloor. "The Failure of Relational Database, the Rise of Object Technology and the Need for the Hybrid Database," (2004), http://www.intersystems.com/cache/technology/whitepapers/baroudi_bloor.pdf (accessed 30 August 2006).

8. Bloor. 5.

9. Bloor. 5.

10. John F Sowa, "Existential Graphs: MS 514 by Charles Sanders Peirce," http://www.jfsowa.com/peirce/ms514.htm. (accessed 27 September 2006).

Chapter 4

1. CP 6.168

2. CP 5.674

3. Winfred P. Lehmann and Eugene D. Pendergraft. "Dynamic Adaptive Data Base Management Study, Third Quarterly Progress Report, 16 November 1966–15 February 1967," Linguistics Research Center, (University of Texas at Austin: 01 May 1967. 3–11). This study was accessed through The

Defense Technical Information Center, AD653640: http://www.dtic.mil/ (accessed 20 September 2006).

4. Jane Mazzagatti. "A Computer Memory Resident Data Structure Based on the Phaneron of C. S. Peirce." 16–21 July 2006. 14th International Conference on Conceptual Structures. Aalborg University, Denmark. 17 July 2006. http://www.iccs-06.hum.aau.dk/ (Accessed 29 September 2006).

5. Winfred P. Lehmann and Eugene D. Pendergraft. "Machine Language Translation Study," Linguistics Research Center, (University of Texas at Austin: 01 May 1966). This study was accessed through The Defense Technical Information Center, AD0635505: http://www.dtic.mil/ (accessed 17 October 2006).

6. Charles Hartshorne and Paul Weiss, eds. "Collected Papers of Charles Sanders Peirce." (Cambridge, Massachusetts: Harvard University Press, Vols. I-IV, 1931–35). And A. Burks, ed. "Collected Papers of Charles Sanders Peirce." (Cambridge, Massachusetts: Harvard University Press, Edited by, Vols. VII-VIII, 1958).

7. ____ The Peirce Edition Project, ed. "Writings of Charles S. Peirce: A Chronological Edition." (Bloomington: Indiana University Press, 1982).

8. Eugene Pendergraft, "The Future's Voice: Intelligence Based on Pragmatic Logic." Creative Intelligence Incorporated. Unpublished, June 1993. 6.

9. Past Masters, InteLex Corp. (Charlottesville, VA). The Collected Papers of Charles S. Peirce," Edited by Charles Hartshorne and Paul Weiss (vols. 1–6), and Arthur Burks (vols. 7–8) and published by Harvard University Press. Licensed from Harvard.

10. CP 5.469

11. Wikipedia   contributors,   "Pixelation,"   *Wikipedia,   The   Free Encyclopedia,* http://en.wikipedia.org/w/index. php?title=Pixelation&oldid=107985687 (accessed 26 July 2006).

12. CP 1.346

13. Jane Mazzagatti. Patent 7,158,975, (2007) and Patent 6,961,733, (2005). Applications 20070038654, (2007), 20060114255, (2006), 20060101048,

(2006), 20060101018 (2006), 20060100845 (2006), 20060074947 (2006), 20060074939 (2006), 20050165772 (2005), 20050165749 (2005), 20050076011 (2005), and 20040181547 (2004).

14. CP 3.284

Chapter 5

1. Kenneth Laine Ketner, and Arthur F. Stewart. "The History of Computer Design: Charles Sanders Peirce and Marquand's Logical Machines." The Princeton University Library Chronicle 45 (1984) 211.

2. Wikipedia contributors, "Computer," *Wikipedia, The Free Encyclopedia,* http://en.wikipedia.org/w/index. php?title=Computer&oldid=113495317 (accessed March 10, 2007).

Chapter 6

1. T. S. Eliot. Choruses from the Rock. 1934

2. Charles S Hardwick, ed. *Semiotics and Signifiers: The Correspondence between Charles S. Peirce and Victoria Lady Welby.* From a letter to Lady Welby dated May 20, 1911. The Press of Arisbe Associates, Elsah, Illinois. 2001. 141.

3. Richard Hooker. "Greek Philosophy: Aristotle." 1996. http:// www.wsu.edu:8080/~dee/GREECE/ARIST.HTM (accessed 05 May 2005).

4. R.L Ackoff, "From Data to Wisdom," Journal of Applied Systems Analysis, 16 (1989) 3–9.

5. Gene Bellinger, Durval Castro, and Anthony Mills. "Data, Information, Knowledge, Wisdom." *Mental Model Musings*, 2004. http://www.systems-thinking.org/dikw/dikw.htm (accessed 12 June 2005).

6. Sharon Allen. *Data Modeling for Everyone.* (Curlingstone, 2002), Chapter 1.

7. Wikipedia contributors, "Dimensional database," *Wikipedia, The Free Encyclopedia,* http://en.wikipedia.org/w/ index.php?title=Dimensional_database&oldid=110717275 (accessed 19 September 2005)/

8.   ___ "Data Structure," *Webopedia*. http://www.webopedia.com/TERM/D/data_structure.html (accessed 11 June 2005).

9.   Robin Bloor. "The Failure of Relational Database, The Rise of Object Technology and the Need for the Hybrid Database." Baroudi Bloor International Incorporated. (2004). 5. http://www.intersystems.com/cache/technology/whitepapers/baroudi_bloor.pdf (accessed 02 September 2005).

10. Bloor. 6.

11. John C. Worsley and Joshua D. Drake (eds.). *Practical PostgreSQL*. (Sebastopol, CA: O'Reilly Media, 2002). 35–37.

12. Bloor. 5.

13. Thomas H. Cormen, Charles E. Leiserson, and Ronald L. Rivest. *Introduction to Algorithms*. (Cambridge Massachusetts: McGraw Hill, 1997).

14. Russell Kay. "Data Cubes." *Computerworld*. March 29, 2004. http://www.computerworld.com/databasetopics/data/story/0,10801,91640,00.html (accessed 09 September 2005).

15. CP 7.459

Chapter 7

1.   CP 8.119

2.   ___ "Evidence Based Medicine," *Suny Downstate Medical Center*. 2001. http://servers.medlib.hscbklyn.edu/ebm/toc.html (accessed 29 June 2005).

3.   ___ "Data and Relationships," FunctionX, 2004, http://www.functionx.com/vcsharp/databases/datarelations.htm (accessed 14 July 2005).

4.   James D. Savage, "The 'Rule Book' of Logical Data Modeling," *Teradata Magazine Online*, [March 2005, http://www.teradata.com/t/page/132175/ (accessed 17 August 2005).

5.   Bill Palace, "What is Data Mining," Technology Note for Anderson Graduate School of Management at UCLA, 1996, http://www.anderson.ucla.edu/faculty/jason.frand/teacher/technologies/palace/datamining.htm   Spring 1996 (Accessed 12 August 2005).

6. ___ 2005 Top Ten Program, Winter Corporation, http://www. wintercorp.com/ (accessed 29 November 2005).

7. Graham Williams, "Apriori: Association Analysis," *Data Mining Desktop Survival Guide*, Togaware.com. http://datamining.togaware.com/survivor/ Apriori.html (accessed March 7, 2007).

8. Palace. (Accessed 12 August 2005).

Chapter 8

1. CP 1.231

2. Philip P Wiener, ed. "Classification of the Sciences," *Dictionary of the History of Ideas*, http://etext.lib.virginia.edu/cgi-local/DHI/ot2www-dhi?specfile=/ texts/english/dhi/dhi. o2w&act=text&offset=3439410&query=classification+&tag=CLASSIFICA-TION+OF+THE+SCIENCES (accessed 20 July 2005).

3. Wikipedia contributors, "Social construction," *Wikipedia, The Free Encyclopedia*, http://en.wikipedia.org/w/ index.php?title=Social_construction&oldid=113950155 (accessed 10 March 2007).

4. David T Kirkpatrick, "An Essay on Taxonomy and the Genus *Pelusios*." Originally published in Reptile & Amphibian Magazine, March/April 1995, 32–40, http://www.unc.edu/~dtkirkpa/stuff/pel.html (accessed 19 September 2005).

5. Kirkpatrick.

6. Leslie A. Pray, "Modern Phylogeneticists Branch Out." *The Scientist*. 17 (June 2, 2003): 11, 35.

7. Judith Rosen, "'Hard' Science and 'Soft' Science," 7 Jul 2005 http:// panmere.com/rosen/mhout/msg03261.html (accessed 12 December 2005).

8. Weiner.

9. Charles S.Claxton and Patricia H. Murrell. "Learning Styles". ERIC Digest. 1988 ERIC Identifier ED301143. Refers to a paper by P. Kirby. Cognitive

Style, Learning, and Transfer Skill Acquisition, Information Series No. 195, Ohio State University, National Center for Research in Vocational Education, Columbus, OH 1979.

10. CP 1.561

11. ___ "Learning Styles," *Litsource*. Pikes Peak, Adult Literacy Program, March 2003. http://www.ppld.org/AboutYourLibrary/Volunteer/LitSourceNewsletters/2003%20-%20March.pdf (accessed 19 September 2005).

12. Nathan Houser and Christian Kloesel, Introduction to *The Essential Peirce*, Vol. 1 http://www.iupui.edu/~peirce/ep/ep1/heads/ep1heads.htm (accessed 29 September 2005).

13. CP 1.561

14. Kelly A. Parker, *The Continuity of Peirce's Thought*. (Nashville: Vanderbilt University Press, 1998) 61.

15. CP 1.354

16. Morris R. Cohen, *Chance, Love, and Logic: Philosophical Essays*, (Lincoln: University of Nebraska Press 1998). Contains Charles Peirce's articles from the philosophical review "The Monist."

17. CP 1.364

18. CP 1.355

19. Houser and Kloesel.

20. Houser and Kloesel.

21. Houser and Kloesel.

22. Charles S Hardwick, ed. *Semiotics and Signifiers: The Correspondence between Charles S. Peirce and Victoria Lady Welby*. From a letter to Lady Welby dated May 20, 1911. The Press of Arisbe Associates, Elsah, Illinois. 2001. 8, 134.

23. Hardwick. 134.

24. Parker. xv.

25. CP 1.203

26. CP 1.204

27. Parker. 34.

28. CP 1.204

29. Parker. 34.

30. Parker. 34.

31. Parker. 34.

32. Parker. 34.

33. Parker. 35 (paraphrasing CSP in CP 1.208).

34. Parker. 35–36.

35. Parker. 36.

36. Menno Hulswit,. "Natural Classes and Causation." *Digital Encyclopedia of Charles S. Peirce.* http://www.digitalpeirce.fee.unicamp.br/hulswit/p-nathul.htm (accessed 10 March 2007).

37. Susan Haack, "Extreme Scholastic Realism: Its Relevance to Philosophy of Science Today," *Transactions of the Charles S. Peirce Society.* XXVII, No. 1, (Winter 1992) 32.

38. CP 1.204

39. Bill Palace, "What is Data Mining," Technology Note for Anderson Graduate School of Management at UCLA, 1996, http://www.anderson.ucla.edu/faculty/jason.frand/teacher/technologies/palace/datamining.htm Spring 1996 (Accessed 12 August 2005).

Chapter 9

1. CP 5.309

2.   CP 7.392

3.   Herb Edelstein,. "Data Mining: Exploiting the Hidden Trends in Your Data." Adapted from a report "Data Mining: Products, Applications, Technology." Two Crows Corporation. http://www.twocrows.com/ (accessed 10 October 2006).

4.   ___ "Market Basket Analysis," *Megaputer Intelligence*. 2005. http://www.megaputer.com/products/pa/algorithms/ba.php3 (accessed 15 January 2006).

5.   Sally Jo Cunningham and Frank E. "Market Basket Analysis of Library Circulation Data." (1999) *Proc Sixth International Conference on Neural Information Processing (ICONIP'99),*Volume II, edited by T. Gedeon, P. Wong, S. Halgamuge, N. Kasabov, D. Nauck and K. Fukushima, Perth, Western Australia, pp 825–830. http://www.cs.waikato.ac.nz/~ml/publications/1999/99SJC-EF-Market-Basket.pdf (accessed 2 February 2006).

6.   Edelstein. "Data Mining."

Chapter 10

1.   CP 6.320

2.   Pak Chung Wong, W. Cowley, H. Foote, E. Jurrus, and J.Thomas. "Visualizing Sequential Patterns for Text Mining." http://www.pnl.gov/infoviz/sequential_patterns.pdf

3.   Bill Palace, "What is Data Mining," Technology Note for Anderson Graduate School of Management at UCLA, 1996, http://www.anderson.ucla.edu/faculty/jason.frand/teacher/technologies/palace/datamining.htm   Spring 1996 (Accessed 12 August 2005).

4.   Gorr, Wilpen and R. Harries. "Introduction to crime forecasting." International Journal of Forecasting 19 (2003) 551–555.

Chapter 11

1.   CP 7.392

2. Bill Palace, "What is Data Mining," Technology Note for Anderson Graduate School of Management at UCLA, 1996, http://www.anderson.ucla.edu/faculty/jason.frand/teacher/technologies/palace/datamining.htm Spring 1996 (Accessed 12 August 2005).

3. Palace.

4. Michael Eisen, Paul T. Spellman, Patrick O. Brown, and David Botstein. "Cluster analysis and display of genome-wide expression patterns". *Proceedings National Academy of Science USA.* 95 December 1998. 14863–14868.

5. Robert E Johnson, "The Role of Cluster Analysis in Assessing Comparability Under the U. S. Transfer Pricing Regulations." *Business Economics.* April 2001. http://www.nabe.com/busecon.htm

6. Valdis Krebs, "An Introduction to Social Network Analysis." http://www.orgnet.com/sna.html (accessed 15 March 2006).

7. Christopher McCarty, "Social Network Analysis." *Bureau of Economic and Business Research.* 2003. www.bebr.ufl.edu/Articles/SNA_Encyclopedia_Entry.pdf (accessed 28 March 2006).

8. ___ "Network Analysis Application". *The Network Roundtable at the University of Virginia.* https://webapp.comm.virginia.edu/NetworkRoundtable/NetworkAnalysisApplications/tabid/36/Default.aspx

9. *Network Roundtable.* I came across this organization chart online and emailed Robert Cross. He graciously gave me permission to use this chart and the fictitious information in this book.

10. Smith, M. K. (2003) "Michael Polanyi and tacit knowledge", *the encyclopedia of informal education,* www.infed.org/thinkers/polanyi.htm. 2006. (accessed March 10, 2007).

Chapter 12

1. CP 2.747

2. CP 2.754

3. "Probability," *Answers.com*. Antonyms, Answers Corporation, 2007. http://www.answers.com/topic/probability, (accessed 21 June 2006).

4. Wikipedia contributors, "Poker probability (Texas hold 'em)," *Wikipedia, The Free Encyclopedia,* http://en.wikipedia.org/w/index.php?title=Poker_probability_%28Texas_hold_%27em%29&oldid=113859337 (accessed 20 June 2006).

5. ___ "What do Probabilities Mean?" BBC. 2006. http://www.bbc.co.uk/dna/h2g2/A543043 (accessed 21 June 2006).

6. Simon Newcomb, "Note on the Frequency of Use of the Different Digits in Natural Numbers," *American Journal of Mathematics* 4 (1881) 39.

7. Wikipedia contributors, "Benford's law," *Wikipedia, The Free Encyclopedia,* http://en.wikipedia.org/w/index.php?title=Benford%27s_law&oldid=113637959 (accessed 23 June 2006).

8. CP 2.1

9. CP 2.747

10. CP 2.747

11. CP 2.747

12. ___ "Training a Neural Network," http://dubinserver.colorado.edu/pr/ale/Train.html. (accessed 21 December 2006.

13. Lou Mendelsohn, "Training Neural Networks," *Market Technologies.* http://www.tradertech.com/training.asp (accessed 5 January 2007).

14. "Markov chain." Dictionary.com. *The Free On-line Dictionary of Computing.* Denis Howe. http://dictionary.reference.com/browse/Markov_chain (accessed: 21 December 2006).

15. CP 5.169

Chapter 13

1. CP 1:284

2. Thich Nhat Hanh, "Understanding Our Mind," (Berkeley, California: Parallax Press, 2006) 13.

3. CP 1.1

4. CP 1.354

5. Charles Hartshorne and Paul Weiss, eds., Footnote to CP 1.354.

6. CP 1.354

7. CP 1.354

8. Brent. *Charles Sanders Peirce: A Life*. (Indiana University Press, 1993) 2.

9. Brent. 3.

10. Brent. 3–4.

11. CP 1.284

12. Jane Mazzagatti. Interview with John Zuchero. 18 December 2006.

13. Jeff Hawkins, *On Intelligence*. (New York: Times Books, Henry Holt and Company, 2004) 33–34.

14. Hawkins. 25.

15. Hawkins. 25.

16. Hawkins. 25.

17. Hawkins. 129.

18. Hawkins. 129.

19. Hawkins. 129.

20. Hawkins. 130

21. CP 1.284

22. CP 1.369

23. Wikipedia contributors, "Syllogism," *Wikipedia, The Free Encyclopedia,* http://en.wikipedia.org/w/index.php?title=Syllogism&oldid=113212872 (accessed 19 December 2006).

24. CP 1.369

25. Hawkins. 68.

26. Jane Mazzagatti. Interview with John Zuchero. 18 December 2006.

27. Wikipedia contributors, "Memory-prediction framework," *Wikipedia, The Free Encyclopedia,* http://en.wikipedia.org/w/index.php?title=Memory-prediction_framework&oldid=113360919 (accessed January 12, 2007).

28. Hawkins. 88–89.

29. CP 1.354

30. Gerald M. Edelman, *Bright Air, Brilliant Fire: On the Matter of the Mind.* (New Yourk: Basicbooks 1992) 15.

31. Edelman. 19.

32. Edelman. 109.

33. CP 1.364

34. Edward O. Wilson, *Consilience: the Unity of Knowledge.* (New York: Knopf. 1998) 8.

35. Eric B Baum, *What is Thought?* (Cambridge: Massachusetts Institute of Technology 2004) 8.

36. Baum. 8.

37. Baum 8.

38. CP 1.568

Glossary

1.   Copyright 1998 Mecklermedia Corporation

2.   Copyright 1998 Mecklermedia Corporation

3.   Principia Cybernetica Web 1998 http://pespmc1.vub.ac.
     be/ASC/indexASC.html

4.   Mecklermedia Corporation. Webopedia.com. 1998.

5.   Unberto Eco and Thomas A. Sebeok, eds. *The Sign of Three*. (Indiana Press,
     1983) 8.

6.   Copyright 1998 Mecklermedia Corporation.

7.   Eco. 8.

8.   Kloesgen and Zytkow, "Machine Discovery Terminology." http://atrey.
     karlin.mff.cuni.cz/~doug/magdon/terms.html

9.   Denis Howe, FOLDOC internet dictionary. 1998.

10. Howe

11. Copyright 1998 Mecklermedia Corporation

12. Copyright 1998 Mecklermedia Corporation

13. Howe

Glossary

Abduction

The process by which hypotheses are created, refined, or eliminated. Those that prove useful are kept as "memory" that may then be used to explain experience by induction, or prepare to act in deduction. "Abduction enables us to formulate a general prediction." C.S. Peirce used the following to explain abduction.

All beans from this bag are white.
These beans are white.
These beans are from this bag

Aggregation

Data aggregation is any process in which information is gathered and expressed in a summary form, for purposes such as statistical analysis. For example, daily sales data may be aggregated so as to compute monthly or annual total amounts.

Algorithm

A formula or set of steps for solving a particular problem. To be an algorithm, a set of rules must be unambiguous and have a clear stopping point. Algorithms can be expressed in any language, from natural languages like English or French to programming languages.[1] See also *analytic*.

Analytic

A computer program (or set of programs) which is designed to systematically solve a certain kind of problem. See also, algorithm.

API

See Application Programming Interface

Application Programming Interface

Interfaces by which different parts or modules of software access and communicate with one another.

Artificial Intelligence

The branch of computer science concerned with making computers behave like humans. The term was coined in 1956 by John McCarthy at the Massachusetts Institute of Technology. Artificial intelligence includes expert systems, natural language, neural networks, and robotics.[2]

Associated Rules

The KStore Associated Rules analytic searches for interesting relationships among items in a given data set and returns a list of variable and combinations of variables and their probability of co-occurring with a focus variable. As a practical use of this analytic, associated rules describe events that tend to occur together.

Association

The process of putting together two or more disparate data sets in order to discover unknown relationships or trends that may exist within the data.

Autonomous

Independent, self-contained. Referring to the KStore condition or quality of being self-organizing.

Autopoeisis

The process whereby an organization produces itself. An autopoietic organization is an autonomous and self-maintaining unity which contains component-producing processes. The components, through their interaction, generate recursively the same network of processes that produced them. An autopoietic system is operationally closed and structurally state determined with no apparent inputs and outputs. A cell, an organism, and perhaps a corporation are examples of autopoietic systems.[3]

Bayes Classification

A probability model. Known to come in two forms: naïve and full. The KStore analytic uses the Naïve Bayes probability model. Naïve Bayes is a technique for estimating probabilities of individual feature values, given a class, from data and to then allow the use of these probabilities to classify new records. In spite of their naive design and apparently over-simplified assumptions, naive Bayes classifiers often work very well in complex real-world situations, such as for diagnosis and classification. Independent, self-contained.

Bill and Tom

Jane Mazzagatti's long-lost uncles. When Jane was a child, Uncles Bill and Tom would read to her from Peirce's essay, "The Fixation of Belief."

BI

See Business Intelligence

Business Intelligence (BI)

Business intelligence (BI) is a broad category of applications and technologies for gathering, storing, analyzing, and providing access to data to help enterprise users make better business decisions. BI applications include the activities of decision support systems, query and reporting, online analytical processing (OLAP), statistical analysis, forecasting, and data mining.

Case

The first sign of the sequential event of creating a new sign. See also *Result*.

Case-based reasoning

Technique whereby "cases" similar to the current problem are retrieved and their "solutions" modified to work on the current problem.

Chart Generator

A general KStore method for providing a display of data such as charts and graphs, from an interlocking trees datastore in a graphical display system having a graphic display device. KStore Chart Generator analytic graphs the counts of the fields and values selected.

Class

A set of variable values associated by a common meaning; i.e., variable class = days of the week, values = Monday, Tuesday, Wednesday, Thursday ...

Classification

A systematic arrangement of objects (of any type) into groups or categories according to a set of established criteria.

Identifying one variable value of class of variables, that has the highest probability given a context and a focus.

In KStore, classification is a form of data analysis that can be used to extract models describing important data classes used for making business decisions. For example, a classification model may be built to categorize bank loan applications as either safe or risky. Currently, there are multiple classification analytics in KStore (See also Contexted Classification, Bayes Classification, and Dynamic Decision Tree.)

Class variable

A single variable value; i.e. class variable = Monday

Column

A class.

Column variable

A single variable value.

Connexion

The connection between sequential signs. Contains bi-directional pointers between the case sign node and the new sign node and the result sign node and the new sign node. In the KStore interlocking trees data structure, the connexions are bi-directional pointers that point to, and back from each node.

Constraint

A variable value that limits a data set to only those sequences containing it. A constraint is either a field value or a field name/field value pair that limits a data set to only those records containing it. Constraints are typically one or more field values that determine which records will be isolated for analysis.

Constraint list

A constraint list contains constraints that are variables that limit the records a query will process whereas the focus is a variable value that is the subject of interest, usually within a context defined by a set of constraints. For example, a basic query could return the total number of widgets sold.

Context

A set of records defined by a set of constraint variable values.

Corpus, corpora (pl)

General: a large collection of writings of a specific kind, or on a specific subject.

Cybernetics

Originally the study of biological and artificial control systems, cybernetics has evolved into many disparate areas of study, with research in many disciplines, including computer science, social philosophy and epistemology. In general, cybernetics is concerned with discovering what mechanisms control systems, and, in particular, how systems regulate themselves. The term was first coined by Norbert Weiner in 1943.[4]

Data models

A structure in which a computer program stores persistent information. In a relational database, data models are built from tables. Within a table, information is stored in homogeneous columns, e.g., a column named registration_date would contain information only of the type "date." In KStore data models are built in the interlocking trees data store.

Detailed Design Specification (DDS)

A deliverable that is developed during the Design Phase, which describes how a system is designed based on identifying the functional components.

Deduction

Drawing a conclusion by reasoning. For example,
All beans from this bag are white.
These beans are from this bag
These beans are white.[5]

Distinct Count

A KStore analytic that returns the count of each distinct value in a given data set. With distinct count, duplicates are not counted. Distinct count is used when an exact count is needed. For example, if a sales manager wants to determine the number of items sold by a given salesperson.

Elemental root node

A SIGN-node representing the sensory input from which all other SIGN-nodes are constructed. A set of records defined by a set of constraint variable values.

End Product Node

The final subcomponent node of a sequence, a monad.

Expert System

Programming computers to make decisions in real-life situations (for example, some expert systems help doctors diagnose diseases based on symptoms).[6]

Extensible Markup Language (XML)

A standard for creating markup languages which describe the structure of data. It is not a fixed set of elements like HTML, but rather, it is like SGML (Standard Generalized Markup Language) in that it is a meta-language, or a language for describing languages.

Feedback

Information, results, or calculations returned the user from the KStore engine or analytic via an API.

Field

A class.

Field variable

A single variable value.

Focus

A variable value that is the subject of interest, usually within a context defined by a set of constraints.

Generalization

A logical process in abduction where acts are classified and grouped into new, more abstract groups. The new group is called a class of acts.

Graphical User Interface (GUI)

Any system that uses graphics to represent the functions of a program.

Induction

Reasoning from the particular to the general. C.S. Peirce used the following figure to explain induction:
These beans are from this bag
These beans are white.
All beans from this bag are white.[7]

Intensity variable

A mathematical entity holding at least one unchangeable value (taken from 188a).

Interlocking trees data store

The generalized organization of the KStore interlocking trees data structure. Composed of a continuum of triads, the tree data connects through connexions pointing to signs.

Knowledge Discovery in Databases (KDD)

A form of machine discovery dealing with knowledge discovery processes in databases. KDD applies to the ready data available in all application domains of science and in applied domains of marketing, planning, controlling, etc. Typically, KDD has to deal with inconclusive data, noisy data, and sparse data.[8]

KStore

A set of computer algorithms that can gain knowledge and learn from a corpus of information.

Knowledge base

A collection of knowledge expressed using some formal knowledge representation language. A knowledge base forms part of a knowledge-based system (KBS).[9]

Knowledge management

A distributed hypermedia system for managing knowledge.[10]

Machine learning

The ability of a machine to improve its performance based on previous results.[11]

Market Basket Analysis

Market Basket Analysis is used to determine which products sell together. In data mining, Market Basket Analysis is an algorithm that examines a long list of transactions in order to determine which items are most frequently purchased together. It takes its name from the idea of a person in a supermarket throwing all of his items into a shopping cart (a "market basket"). The results can be useful to any company that sells products, whether it's in a store, a catalog, or directly to the customer.

Mechanized language translation

The ability of a machine or computer to automatically translate one language to another.

Mechanized semiosis

An implementation of the logical processes by which knowledge is created as represented by signs.

Monad

The last SIGN-node of a sequence, representing a complete logical sequence of SIGN-nodes. These monad SIGN-nodes can be used to construct higher level (or more abstract) sequences.

Morphology

The acts governing the internal construction of words.

Neural nets, neural networks

Systems that simulate intelligence by attempting to reproduce the types of physical connections that occur in animal brains.[12]

Path

The sequence of SIGN-nodes depending from a BOT indicator to an end-product SIGN-node.
asCase paths are linked from BOT to EOT and case paths are linked from EOT to BOT—and K paths can be followed in either direction. Use the term K Path when you talk about the entire path without regard for direction. Having said that we could use the same for the relational K paths (the dotted lines)

Peirce, Charles Sanders (1839–1914)

American scientist, philosopher, physicist, mathematician; founder of pragmatism and the primary source of the contemporary philosophical conception of "semiotic" as a general theory of representation and interpretation. The KStore is based on his theories and work.

Phaneron

C. S. Peirce defined Phaneron as the collective total of all that is present to the mind, regardless if it corresponds to anything that is real or not. In the case of field/record or text data, the Phaneron is all of the data available to the KStore engine.

Point of attention

Location of the current K 'position pointer'.

Result

The second sign of the sequential event of creating a new sign. The Result sign represents what is seen or experienced. The result of the sequence of case/result is a new sign. See also *Case*.

SDK

See Software Developers Kit

Semiotics

The science of signs, symbols, and icons.

Sensor

1. The smallest unit that can be represented by a sign node and the foundation for the knowledge structure. C. S. Peirce referred to this as a "prebit."

2. A device used to measure a physical quantity such as temperature, pressure or loudness and convert it into an electronic signal of some kind. Sensors are normally components of some larger electronic system such as a computer control and/or measurement system.

Sensor node

An elemental node that contains values for the smallest data component that can be read into the interlocking trees data structure. In the case of field/record or text data, that would be alphanumeric characters, special characters, and some control elements.

Sign

1. In Semiotics, something that stands for another thing (its object) and which influences its interpreter (its interpretant).

2. In KStore, the elements or sequences of elements that comprise the interlocking tree data structure.

Sign node

A node of the KStore structure—either an elemental or sensor node, or a node representing the sequence of two nodes.

Single Variable Prediction

The Single Variable Prediction analytic returns the probability of a focus variable. The focus variables may be optionally limited by constraints, which are typically one or more values that determine which records will be isolated for analysis. The probability of the focus variable is equal to the number of records containing the focus variable over the total number of records.

Software Developers Kit (SDK)

1. Software provided by a software vendor to allow their products to be used with those of other software vendors.13

2. For KStore it refers to a set of tools developed to support the integration and use of the KStore. Specifically, it will consist of API specification and code, as well as tools to ensure quality and accuracy.

Subcomponent node

In the KStore interlocking data structure, a sub-component node is a new sign node. It is not a beginning of thought (BOT), end-of-thought (EOT), or sensor, but a component of the tree structure that has been formed by the sequence of BOT and sensors.

Triad

The basic building block of the interlocking tress data structure known as KStore. A triad is composed of a case Sign node, a result Sign node, and a new Sign node.

Triadic continuum

The continuous structure composed of triads that form the entire interlocking trees data structure known as the KStore.

Bibliography

Albers, Michael J. and Beth Mazur, ed. (2003). *Content and Complexity*. Mahwah: Lawrence Erlbaum Associates.

Anderson, J. A. (1995). *An Introduction to Neural Networks*. London: The MIT Press.

Baum, Eric B. (2004). *What is Thought?* Cambridge: MIT Press.

Brent, Joseph. (1993). *Charles Sanders Peirce: A Life*. Bloomington: Indiana.

Bundy, Alan, ed. (1997). *Artificial Intelligence Techniques*. Berlin: Springer.

Cobley, Paul and Litza Jansz. (2004). *Introducing Semiotics*. Lanham: Totem Books.

Cohen, Morris R., ed. (1998). *Chance, Love, and Logic*. Lincoln: Bison Books.

Cormen, Thomas H., Charles E. Leiserson, and Ronald L. Rivest. (1997). *Introduction to Algorithms*. Cambridge: The MIT Press.

Dewey, John. (1938). *Logic: The Theory of Inquiry*. New York: Henry Holt and Company.

Dowling, John E. (1998). *Creating Mind: How the Brain Works*. New York: W. W. Norton and Company.

Eco, Umberto and Thomas A. Sebeok, ed. (1983). *The Sign of Three*. Bloomington: Indiana.

Eisele, Carolyn (1979). *Studies in the Scientific and Mathematical Philosophy of C.S. Peirce*, Richard Milton Martin (ed.), The Hague: Mouton.

_____ *Historical Perspectives on Peirce's Logic of Science: A History of Science*, Eisele, Carolyn (ed.), (1985) The Hague: Mouton.

_____ The *New Elements of Mathematics by Charles S. Peirce*, Eisele, Carolyn (ed.), (1976) The Hague: Mouton.

Edelman, Gerald M. (1992). *Bright Air, Brilliant Fire: On the Matter of the Mind*. New York: Basic Books.

Franklin, Stan. (1998). *Artificial Minds*. Cambridge: MIT Press.

Gardner, Howard. (1999). *Intelligence Reframed*. New York: Basic Books.

Haack, Susan. "Extreme Scholastic Realism: Its Relevance to Philosophy of Science Today," *Transactions of the Charles S. Peirce Society*. Vol. XXVII, No. 1, Winter 1992. Pages 19–50.

Han, Jiawei and Micheline Kamber. (2001). *Data Mining: Concepts and Techniques*. San Francisco: Morgan Kaufmann Publishers.

Hardwick, Charles S. (2001). *Semiotic and Significs: The Correspondence between Charles S. Peirce and Victoria Lady Welby*. Elsah: The Press of Arisbe Associates.

Harris, Robert L. (1999). *Information Graphics*. New York: Oxford University Press.

Hawkins, Jeff. (2004). *On Intelligence*. New York Times Books.

Horn, Robert E. (1998). *Visual Language*. Washington: MacroVU, Inc.

Kachigan, Sam Kash. (1991).*Multivariate Statistical Analysis: A Conceptual Introduction*. New York: Radius Press.

Ketner, Kenneth Laine. (1998). *His Glassy Essence*. Nashville: Vanderbilt University Press.

Ketner, Kenneth Laine, ed. (1992). *Reasoning and the Logic of Things*. Cambridge: Harvard University Press.

Ketner, Kenneth Laine and Arthur F. Stewart.(1984). The History of Computer Design: Charles Sanders Peirce and Marquand's Logical Machines. Princeton: The Princeton University Library Chronicle 45.

Kloesel, Christian J. W. (1986). *Writings of Charles S. Peirce: A Chronological Edition*. 3. Bloomington: Indiana University Press.

Kloesel, Christian J. W. (1986). *Writings of Charles S. Peirce: A Chronological Edition*. 4. Bloomington: Indiana University Press.

Kurzweil, Ray. (1999). *The Age of Spiritual Machines*. New York: Viking Penguin.

Mayr, Ernst. (1969). *Principles of Systematic Zoology*. New York: McGraw-Hill Book Company.

Mendenhall, William. (1979). *Introduction to Probability and Statistics*. Belmont: Wadsworth Publishing Company.

Nhat Hanh, Thich. (2006). *Understanding Our Mind*. Berkley: Parallax Press.

Parker, Kelly A. (1998). *The Continuity of Peirce's Thought*. Nashville: Vanderbilt University Press.

Petersen, John V. (2002). *Absolute Beginner's Guide to Databases*. Indianapolis: Que

Pinker, Steven. (1997). *How the Mind Works*. New York: W. W. Norton and Company.

Rucker, Rudy. (1987). *Mind Tools: The Five Levels of Mathematical Reality*. Boston: Houghton Mifflin Company.

Stevens, Charles F. (1966). *Neurophysiology: A Primer*. New York: John Wiley and Sons, Inc.

Tursman, Richard. (1987). *Peirce's Theory of Scientific Discovery*. Bloomington: Indiana University Press.

Wilson, Edward O. (1998). *Consilience: The Unity of Knowledge*. New York: Alfred A Knoff.

Zeidenberg, Matthew. (1990). *Neural Networks in Artificial Intelligence*. New York: Ellis Horwood Limited.

Index

978-0-595-44112-9
0-595-44112-2

www.ingramcontent.com/pod-product-compliance
Lightning Source LLC
Chambersburg PA
CBHW051230050326
40689CB00007B/859